Contents

Background	4–17
Introduction	4
The city and its suburbs	6
History	8
Politics	12
Culture	14

First steps	18–27
Impressions	18

Destination guide	28–131
Manhattan	28
The Bronx	100
Brooklyn	108
Long Island	116
Queens	118
Staten Island	126

Getting away from it all	132–7

Directory	138–89
Shopping	138
Entertainment	142
Children	148
Sport and leisure	150
Food and drink	156
Accommodation	172
Practical guide	176

Index	190–91

Walks

Battery Park – Financial District	30
Chinatown	36
East Village	40
Greenwich Village	46
SoHo	50
St Paul's Chapel – South Street Seaport	54
TriBeCa	58
Central Park	86
Yorkville	98
Brooklyn Heights	110

Maps

New York City	20–21
Lower Manhattan	29
Walk: Battery Park – Financial District	31
Walk: Chinatown	36
Walk: East Village	41
Walk: Greenwich Village	46
Walk: SoHo	50
Walk: St Paul's Chapel – South Street Seaport	55
Walk: TriBeCa	58
Midtown and Upper Manhattan	63
Walk: Central Park	87
Walk: Yorkville	99
Walk: Brooklyn Heights	110
Long Island	117
Subway map	188–9

Features

Festivals and parades	16
New York Harbor	26
Wall Street	32
Village life	42
Ground Zero	61
Manhattan architecture	66
Broadway and Off-Broadway	76
West Side story	84
African Caribbean connection	92
The European influx	106
Brooklyn lifestyle	112
New Amsterdam	124
Sporting life	154
Fast food	160
Nightlife	166

Introduction

Visitors to New York City almost always arrive with certain expectations – residents are constantly rushing about and are rude, everyone living near Central Park is uber-rich, Harlem is a no-man's-land that ought not be visited. The fact is: New York handily challenges most of these assumptions. The city is welcoming, albeit fast-paced, home to people of all ethnicities and walks of life and one of the safest cities in the USA to explore.

While appreciating that sophisticated Manhattan is actually hemmed in by water, visitors may not be prepared for the beautiful views of the wide Hudson and East rivers as they land at John F Kennedy or LaGuardia airports, or cross the many bridges – the George Washington, Brooklyn, Triborough, Verrazano-Narrows, et al. – for which the city is famous.

Tunnels, too, are a feature of New York, linking the outer boroughs with Manhattan. Within the space of less than a minute you can leave one urban scene and emerge into another that is quite different. There is an area of 787sq km (304sq miles) to discover, much of it free, or costing no more than a few dollars.

The city – with perhaps the exception of Wall Street and South Street Seaport – is easy to navigate due to a systematic grid of streets going east to west and avenues aligned north to south. Explore on foot, or get where you need to go via the city's intricate network of subways, buses and trains.

Urban renewal has been a theme since the early 1990s and the city is devoting its resources to the construction of 'greenways' – hundreds of kilometres of landscaped bike paths and wide walking paths to accommodate the increasing 'go green' attitude of New Yorkers. In fact, Broadway, between Times Square–42nd Street and Herald Square–34th Street, has been transformed into a fashionable, more pedestrian-friendly thoroughfare due to the addition of the greenway.

When planning a trip to New York City, many visitors can't help but wonder what's changed since 11 September 2001, when the skyline was transformed in a matter of moments by the terrorist attack that brought down the soaring twin towers of the World Trade Center. While those iconic structures are gone, new buildings have been erected in the

As one of th

a

Thomas

For more than 135 years our
oks have unlocked the secrets
stinations around the world,
ng with travellers a wealth of
experience and a passion for travel.

**Rely on Thomas Cook as your
travelling companion on your next trip
and benefit from our unique heritage.**

Thomas Cook **traveller** guides

NEW YORK
Eric & Ruth Bailey

Your travelling companion since 1873

Thomas
Cook

Written by Eric and Ruth Bailey, updated by Andrea M. Rotondo
Original photography by Paul Kenward

Published by Thomas Cook Publishing
A division of Thomas Cook Tour Operations Limited.
Company Registration no. 3772192 England
The Thomas Cook Business Park, Unit 9, Coningsby Road,
Peterborough PE3 8SB, United Kingdom
Email: books@thomascook.com, Tel: + 44 (0) 1733 416477
www.thomascookpublishing.com

Produced by Cambridge Publishing Management Ltd
Unit 2, Burr Elm Court, Caldecote CB23 7NU
www.cambridgepm.co.uk

ISBN: 978-1-84848-323-1

© 2002, 2005, 2007 Thomas Cook Publishing
This fourth edition © 2010
Text © Thomas Cook Publishing
Maps © Thomas Cook Publishing/PCGraphics (UK) Limited
Transport map © Communicarta Limited

Series Editor: Karen Beaulah
Production/DTP: Steven Collins

Printed and bound in Spain by GraphyCems

Cover photography: © Simeone Giovanni/SIME-4Corners Images

vicinity and a permanent memorial is nearing completion.

That part of town may look a bit different, but visitors will still thrill at recognising landmarks they have never seen except on the big screen – the Empire State Building, the Statue of Liberty, Tiffany's, Brooklyn Bridge. And with the aid of this book, it should be easy to find a vast range of interesting, often exciting, things to see and do in the world's most glamorous city.

'This is the first sensation of life in New York – you feel that the Americans have practically added a new dimension to space. They move almost as much on the perpendicular as on the horizontal plane. When they find themselves a little crowded, they simply tilt a street on end and call it a skyscraper.' **WILLIAM ARCHER**, 1899

'New York appears to be a great city in a great hurry. The average street pace must surely be 40 miles an hour.' **CECIL BEATON**, 1938

'Something's always happening here. If you're bored in New York, it's your own fault.' **MYRNA LOY**, 1987

Introduction

Iconic skyline – the Empire State Building (left) and the Chrysler Building

The city and its suburbs

The sprawl that is New York City covers a group of islands in New York Bay, where the Hudson River enters the Atlantic Ocean. It lies at the conjunction of three states: southeastern New York, southwestern Connecticut and northeastern New Jersey. The Narrows, a strait between Staten Island and Brooklyn, separates the upper and lower parts of the bay.

At the head of the upper bay is Manhattan Island, 21km (13 miles) long, up to 4km (2½ miles) wide and covering 60sq km (23sq miles). The island is separated from mainland America by the Hudson River to the west, the East River to the east, and the Harlem River and Spuyten Duyvil Creek in the northeast. Strictly speaking, though, the East River is a strait linking Long Island Sound and New York Bay, but it looks and smells like a river, so who is going to argue? With the city's access to both the Hudson and East rivers, it's no wonder there's as much action on the water as on land. Visitors will find ferry crossings and piers for day-trip sightseeing vessels and ocean-going cruise ships alike.

New York is the largest city in the USA and one of the world's most populous urbanised areas. It is not, as some people think, the capital of the USA. That would be Washington, DC. It's not even the capital of the state that also bears its name. That distinction goes to Albany. But it is unquestionably the country's cultural, communications, corporate and financial capital, and it takes a leading position in the fields of politics, education, industry, technology, commerce and transport. This is where political leaders and titans of business meet to solve the country's – and sometimes the world's – most pressing issues.

The city's international stature was acknowledged after World War II when it was chosen as the site of the United Nations headquarters. The complex is on First Avenue between 42nd and 48th streets, overlooking the East River, and is considered international territory.

Metropolitan New York consists of five boroughs – the Bronx, Brooklyn, Manhattan, Queens and Staten Island – covering a total of 787sq km (304sq miles). Most northerly of the boroughs and the only one on the mainland, the Bronx has 1.4 million inhabitants and, in the South Bronx, a fearsome reputation for violence (although the area is less dangerous now than it was in the 1980s and early 1990s). Settled in the 17th century by a Danish immigrant named Johannes Bronck, the Bronx today has a rich Italian heritage, splendid botanical gardens, the former homes of writers Edgar Allan Poe and Mark Twain and, for baseball fans, the new Yankee Stadium.

Brooklyn, at the western tip of Long Island, became New York's first suburb when it was annexed by the city in 1898. With more than 2½ million citizens – 1 million more than Manhattan – it has cobbled streets, about 600 buildings more than a century old and a spectacular view of Manhattan.

Queens, named to honour the wife of England's King Charles II, is the home of John F Kennedy International Airport and LaGuardia Airport.

New Yorkers tend to think it dull, but Queens has a lively Greek community – the largest outside Greece – a South American quarter and thriving film studios. It's also the home field for the New York Mets, who play at the new Citi Field.

Staten Island is connected to Brooklyn by the 1,298m (4,260ft) Verrazano-Narrows Bridge. Most visitors, however, take the 20-minute Staten Island Ferry trip from Manhattan that gives wonderful views of skyscrapers and the Statue of Liberty. The island's attractions are scattered.

Manhattan is the place where the majority of visitors spend most of their time. Here are the famous skyscrapers, the museums, world-renowned boutiques and the Broadway theatres. Here are the places known from a hundred films.

The city and its suburbs

Manhattan, looking towards the Bronx

History

1492   Columbus discovers America.

1524   Italian explorer Giovanni da Verrazano sails into New Harbor and discovers the islands that became New York City.

1609   Englishman Henry Hudson, working for the Dutch East India Company, cruises up the river that now bears his name.

Statue of Liberty

1625   The Dutch establish the first permanent settlement in Lower Manhattan, named New Amsterdam.

1626   Governor Peter Minuit buys Manhattan from the Indians for trinkets worth about $24.

1636   Settlers buy what is now Brooklyn from the Indians.

1641   Johannes Bronck buys part of what is now the Bronx from the Indians, who drive settlers from Staten Island.

1643   First permanent settlement established in Flushing, Queens.

1653   New Amsterdam receives charter as municipal government. Governor Peter Stuyvesant has a wall built river-to-river to keep out British trade rivals. Where it stood is now Wall Street.

1664   The British take the city without a fight and rename it after the Duke of York, brother of King Charles II.

1673	The Dutch recapture the city and call it New Orange.
1674	The British gain permanent control of the city and province, and name both New York.
1776	Declaration of Independence is signed; battles take place between Americans and British. The British occupy all of what is present-day New York.
1783	Revolutionary War ends and colonies gain independence. New York becomes capital of the USA for a brief period.
1792	Congress decides to issue stock to pay for the Revolutionary War, forming the basis of the New York Stock Exchange.
1813	Robert Fulton starts a ferry service between Manhattan and Brooklyn.
1820	Census puts population at 123,706 – New York is the nation's largest city.
1825	New York flourishes as a port. Large-scale immigration from Europe begins.

1858	Shanty-town slums in Central Manhattan are torn down to create Central Park.
1861	New York joins with 23 northern states to fight the South in the Civil War.
1883	Brooklyn Bridge opens.
1892	Beginning of the era of mass immigration through Ellis Island, where 17 million new citizens were processed into the country over 62 years.
1898	New York is officially formed with five boroughs united under one municipality – the new city is the world's second largest, with a population of 3½ million.
1902	The Flatiron Building, Madison Square, heralds the age of the skyscraper.
1920	Prohibition ushers in the age of speakeasies and gangsters.
1929	The Wall Street Crash marks the start of the Great Depression.

1931	The Empire State Building – the world's tallest at the time – is completed.
1939	Opening of LaGuardia Airport, named after Mayor Fiorello LaGuardia.
1940	Rockefeller Center opens.
1941	Lights of Manhattan dimmed as USA enters World War II.
1952	United Nations meets at new headquarters overlooking the East River.
1973	World Trade Center opens.
1986	Statue of Liberty centenary celebrated.
1988	World Financial Center opens.
1990	New York's first black mayor, David Dinkins, takes office.
1992	Ellis Island reopens as a museum of immigration.
1993–2001	Rudolph Giuliani elected 107th mayor of New York City, his term distinguished by a reduction in crime of almost 50 per cent.
2001	Hillary Clinton is elected Democratic senator from New York, the first ever former first lady to assume this political office.
11 Sept 2001	Two jet airliners smash into the World Trade Center. The terrorist strike destroys the towers and several buildings in the immediate vicinity, killing approximately 2,750 people.
2002	Michael Bloomberg is elected 108th mayor of New York City. He serves a second term in 2005 and a third in 2009.
2004	The cornerstone is laid for the Freedom Tower on the site where the World Trade Center once stood.
2006	Final design for Freedom Tower is unveiled.
2008	Mayor Bloomberg fights to amend New York City's mayoral term limit laws and wins.
2011	National September 11 Memorial & Museum is set to open to the public on 11 September 2011.

Rockefeller Plaza is a business and entertainment hub in the heart of New York

Politics

Some people say New York is ungovernable, and forecasts of the city's death from fiscal failure have been made at regular intervals since the 19th century. In the 1930s, control of public services passed from the five boroughs to the mayor of New York, and since then there has been a constant, often heated, debate between the proponents of centralisation and those who want power handed back to the boroughs.

The city's highly centralised system of government places considerable power in the hands of its mayor, who is chosen by a city-wide electorate for a term of four years. The mayor has wide executive discretion – and a strong veto – and plays a major role in budget-making. He has the authority to organise and reorganise nine administrative agencies, including the police and fire departments, whose heads he can hire and fire.

The city comptroller, similarly elected, is another powerful figure, whose job is to recommend financial policies and advise the mayor and city council on budget preparations.

New York's policy-making powerhouse is the Board of Estimate, which oversees the budget, as well as franchises, planning matters, public improvements and city-owned property. The board consists of the mayor, comptroller and president of the city council, each with two votes, and the five borough presidents who have one vote each. In 1989, the US Supreme Court ruled that this system was unconstitutional, and since then the city has been trying to develop a more acceptable way of conducting its affairs.

Calls for decentralisation have been growing stronger since the late 1960s, when fiscal problems worsened as many middle-class people began to move out, and the city's tax base began to shrink. Debts mounted to $3.3 billion by 1975. Massive cuts in services, jobs and education helped restore order by 1981.

New York is no longer as bustling as the beaver on its municipal seal might suggest. Important businesses have been moving out, and many people who work in the city, using its facilities, now live and pay taxes elsewhere. Public services and amenities, and the quality of life have certainly been downgraded since the 1960s.

Politically, the city is strongly Democrat. About 70 per cent of registered voters are said to be

Democrats, and 13 per cent Republicans. Yet, the public more often than not elects a Republican for mayor.

The mayoral seat has been occupied by a varied cast, some good, some rotten, many colourful. Among the most popular were Fiorello LaGuardia, nicknamed 'the Little Flower', who cracked down on crooks in a 12-year reign during the 1930s and 1940s, and Ed Koch, the no-nonsense incumbent from 1977 to 1990.

LaGuardia's background – he was a Protestant with an Italian father and a Jewish mother – served as a symbol of the mixed heritages of the citizens he subsequently led. A Republican, he was elected mayor in 1933, and was the first to serve three consecutive terms. He brought about big improvements in slum clearance, public housing and municipal amenities, flamboyantly waged war on crime and corruption – and endeared himself to New Yorkers by reading comics over the radio. Mayor Ed Koch was in many ways a latter-day LaGuardia and also served three terms. His third term ended amid a series of corruption scandals.

He was succeeded by David Dinkins, the first black mayor, and in 1993 by Rudolph Giuliani, lauded for his singular role in reducing New York's crime rate by half of what it had become. The FBI now recognises it as one of the safest large cities in the USA.

In 2002 Michael Bloomberg, a self-made billionaire, succeeded Giuliani as mayor and was re-elected in 2005 for a further four years. In 2008 he petitioned for extended mayoral term limits, ran for office and was once again elected mayor in 2009. Bloomberg was a Democrat until 2001 when he switched allegiance to the Republican Party. In 2007 he became an Independent and remains one to this day. Taking control of the city at a time of financial uncertainty, Bloomberg has tightened the city's budgetary belt and has made a habit of finding ways to do more with less money.

City Hall has been the backdrop for New York's controversial, turbulent and colourful political scene

Culture

New York's rich cultural diversity and its people's liberal attitudes towards the arts and education are no doubt due to standards and aspirations imported by the thousands of immigrants who poured into the city from all over the world 'yearning to be free'. New York may have been the melting pot, but the newcomers themselves were the vital ingredients that were to form its enduring cultural amalgam. It is perhaps one of the greatest cultural centres on earth.

Until the Erie Canal opened in 1825, providing a direct link with the Great Lakes, New York was merely another slowly developing city on the Atlantic seaboard. But with goods and produce flowing to and from the American heartlands, it soon overtook Boston and Philadelphia to become the nation's major seaport. As its wealth increased, immigrants began to arrive in ever-larger waves, bringing with them new ideas as well as new hopes. The Germans and the Irish were the first to arrive in large numbers, followed by Italians and refugees from Eastern Europe, including many Jews. In 1884 immigrants began arriving from the Near and Far East.

Each group of newcomers settled mainly with their own kind, and the city soon had recognisable ethnic communities: Chinatown and Little Italy, Jews in the Lower East Side, the Germans in Yorkville. It is a process that has continued to a large extent to the present day: the African Americans in Harlem, Greeks in Astoria, Puerto Ricans in the South Bronx, Arabs along Brooklyn's Atlantic Avenue and East Indians in Lower Manhattan.

Each ethnic group has had a profound effect on the city's cultural development. Music, musical comedy, the big Broadway musical show; the short story and the long novel; drama, dance, film, art, architecture – it all adds up to a culture not only characteristically American, but also unique to New York.

Although New York has always been a solid enclave of capitalism, with many of its leading citizens of the past unashamedly – and sometimes ruthlessly and illegally – on the make, there have been philanthropists too, benefactors who have endowed art galleries, concert halls, museums, schools and universities. Some of its early politicians set out to determine that in education, at least, everyone had a more or less equal chance.

To this day, New York is unique among US cities in providing public education through to university level. The City University of New York has over 400,000 students at 23 colleges across the city. For more than a century, university tuition was free to New York residents. Fees were imposed only as recently as 1976, when the city found itself in deep financial trouble.

The city's Public Library, on Fifth Avenue, is one of the world's largest research libraries, with access to over 43 million items.

Today, New York has more theatres, concert halls, art galleries and museums than you will find anywhere else in the USA. During the cooler months of the year, some 39 theatres are open on Broadway and in the West 40s and 50s streets. Off-Broadway theatres, mostly in Greenwich Village and Chelsea, number about 200.

The five boroughs are served by about 400 cinemas, ranging from the Radio City Music Hall, seating up to 6,200, to small houses specialising in art films. The city has about 125 commercial art galleries, in addition to the major institutions with their world-renowned collections.

Chinatown is only one ingredient in the rich cultural mix of this city

Festivals and parades

Street parades are a way of life in New York. Periodically, one faction or another makes its presence felt in a chunk of Fifth Avenue or some other location. The first major event after Christmas is the Chinese New Year, celebrated in January or February on the first full moon after 19 January. Dragons, firecrackers, elaborate costumes and the banishment of evil spirits are features of the pageantry centred on Mott Street.

The biggest procession is the St Patrick's Day Parade on 17 March. Americans claiming the merest drop of Irish blood converge from all over the nation. Manhattan bars are packed and the air is loud with pipe and brass band music. Columbus Day, American Independence Day, Memorial and Thanksgiving days warrant huge turnouts, too.

The Greeks celebrate their Independence Day with decorated

Street vendors at the Feast of San Gennaro in Little Italy

Chinese New Year celebrations

1969 when a Christopher Street riot paved the way for the gay rights movement.

Taste of Times Square – a food festival with music and dance held on 25 June – celebrates the vibrant street life of this city.

The museums have their day on the second Tuesday in June when, between 6pm and 9pm, the Museum Mile Festival allows visitors entry into nine museums free of charge, with plenty of outdoor music and art demonstrations for those who prefer to stay outdoors.

In autumn the New Yorker Festival, a literary festival, is held at many locations, where visitors can mingle and share brunch with writers, editors and artists.

Macy's Thanksgiving Day Parade with its amazing floats is an American institution, broadcast live across the nation. New York knows how to throw a party!

floats in Fifth Avenue, usually in April, or in May if the day falls during the Orthodox Lent. The legendary Easter Parade provides an excuse to show off flamboyant, often home-made millinery. Everyone gets a generous taste of ethnic foods at the Ninth Avenue International Festival in May. Little Italy has two festivals, commemorating San Gennaro for ten days in September, with street stalls, music and fast food, and St Anthony of Padua for two weeks in June. Each festival involves bearing a saint's statue through the streets.

The Gay Pride Parade in June, with the accent on drag, marks the day in

Childhood can be magic in the city

Impressions

'New York is an ugly city, a dirty city. Its climate is a scandal, its politics are used to frighten children, its traffic is madness, its competition is murderous. But there is one thing about it – once you have lived in New York and it has become your home, no place else is good enough.'

JOHN STEINBECK, 1953

The city layout

Manhattan Island's layout is straightforward, mainly following a gridiron plan, with avenues and streets laid at right angles to each other – the avenues running north and south, and the streets east and west. Starting in the east, the avenues are numbered from First to Twelfth. Street numbers increase from south to north. The other boroughs do not have this rigid gridiron layout.

On the New York City subway

Transport

From the days of the first technicolour films, the yellow cab has been an enduring symbol of New York City. The archetypal cab driver – laconic, lugubrious, tossing a strangled bon mot over his right shoulder as he wrestles with an oversized steering wheel – remains a monument to supreme indifference in the face of travel stress. A 15 per cent tip is expected.

The subway, New York's 1,162km (722-mile) rail system (one of the world's most complicated underground systems), is cheap and comprehensive, but has a firmly established image of dirt and danger. Neither aspect is entirely true. The graffiti-covered trains have all but disappeared, and both plain-clothes and uniformed transit police are ubiquitous. Nevertheless, the watchword at all times is 'Be careful'.

Thanks to Manhattan's frequent traffic jams, bus travel can provide leisurely sightseeing, but you can bet your last nickel that a gridlock will occur.

Yellow cabs lining up outside John F Kennedy International Airport

Traffic jams are no problem for the Staten Island Ferry (*see p126*), New York's free sightseeing trip – a 20-minute voyage with great views of Manhattan and New York Harbor.

Another inexpensive and exciting experience is the Roosevelt Island Aerial Tramway (completely modernised and renovated in 2010), which crosses the East River from Second Avenue/60th Street. In the film classic *King Kong*, it was the tramway's cars that were given such a hard time by that prototype New York mugger, King Kong.

Hazard lights

Being a pedestrian in New York can be hazardous. At intersections, illuminated signs order you to either 'Don't Walk' or 'Walk'. If it says 'Don't Walk', don't walk. If it says 'Walk', don't walk – until you have checked that you are not about to be mown down by a vehicle just behind you turning right.

Subway safety

Some 4.5 million people use the subway every day. Others are appalled at the idea of using it at all and warn against it. Unscathed visitors sometimes

Ignore these signs at your peril – walking can be a blood sport in New York

New York City

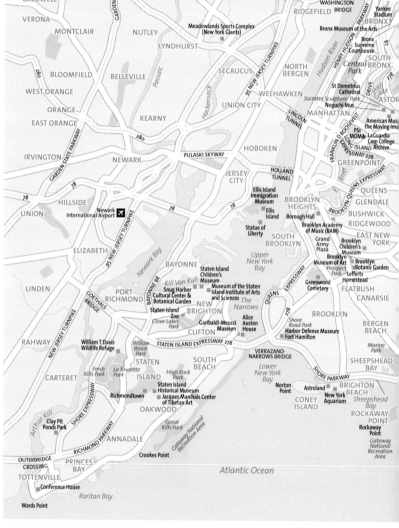

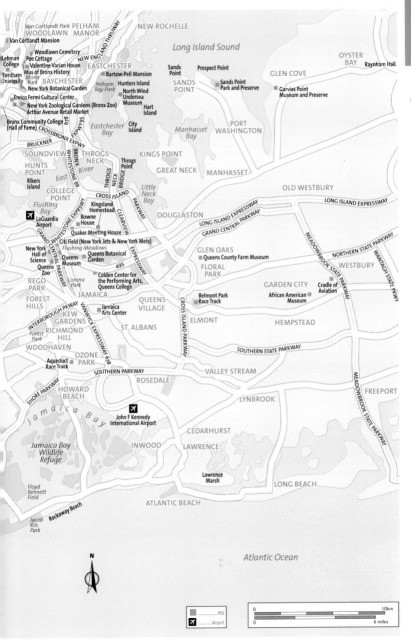

Van Cortlandt Park PELHAM
WOODLAWN MANOR   NEW ROCHELLE
Van Cortlandt Mansion   Long Island Sound   OYSTER
                                                                                                      BAY   Raynham Hall
Lehman   Woodlawn Cemetery   GLEN COVE
College   Poe Cottage   EASTCHESTER   Sands   Prospect Point
          Valentine Varian House   Point
Fordham   Mus of Bronx History   Bartow-Pell Mansion   SANDS   Sands Point
University Bronx   BAYCHESTER   Pelham   Hunters Island   POINT   Park and Preserve   Garvies Point
          Park   New York Botanical Garden   Bay Park   North Wind   Museum and Preserve
Enrico Fermi Cultural Center   Undersea
      New York Zoological Gardens (Bronx Zoo)   Museum   Hart
      Arthur Avenue Retail Market   Island
Bronx Community College   PORT
(Hall of Fame)   CROSSBRONX EXPWY Eastchester   City   Manhasset   WASHINGTON
                                    Bay   Island   Bay
    BRUCKNER
SOUNDVIEW   THROGS   BRONX Throgs   KINGS POINT
HUNTS   NECK   River   Point
POINT   East   THROGS   GREAT NECK   MANHASSET   OLD WESTBURY
Rikers   River   NECK   LONG ISLAND EXPRESSWAY
Island   COLLEGE   BRIDGE   Little
      POINT   CROSS ISLAND   Neck
Flushing   Kingsland   PARKWAY   Bay
 Bay   Homestead   CLEARVIEW
LaGuardia   Bowne   DOUGLASTON   LONG ISLAND EXPRESSWAY
Airport   House   GRAND CENTRAL PARKWAY   NORTHERN STATE PARKWAY
      Quaker Meeting House   EXPRESSWAY   WANTAGH STATE PARKWAY
New York   Citi Field (New York Jets & New York Mets)
Hall of   Flushing Meadows   GLEN OAKS   WESTBURY
Science   Queens   Queens Botanical   Queens County Farm Museum   MEADOWBROOK STATE PARKWAY
Queens   Museum   Garden   495   FLORAL
Zoo   Corona   Colden Center for   PARK   GARDEN CITY   Cradle of
REGO   Park   the Performing Arts,   African American Aviation
PARK   Queens College   Belmont Park   Museum
FOREST   JAMAICA   QUEENS   Race Track
HILLS   KEW   VILLAGE   ELMONT   HEMPSTEAD
       GARDENS   Jamaica
INTERBOROUGH PKWY   Arts Center ST. ALBANS   CROSS ISLAND PARKWAY
Forest   RICHMOND   VANWYCK EXPRESSWAY 678
Park   HILL   SOUTHERN STATE PARKWAY
WOODHAVEN   OZONE
      Aqueduct   PARK
      Race Track   SOUTHERN PARKWAY   VALLEY STREAM   MEADOWBROOK STATE PARKWAY
              ROSEDALE
SHORE PARKWAY   HOWARD   LYNBROOK   FREEPORT
          BEACH
Jamaica Bay   John F Kennedy
              International Airport   CEDARHURST
Jamaica Bay   INWOOD   LAWRENCE
Wildlife
Refuge   Lawrence
                           Marsh   LONG BEACH
Floyd
Bennett
Field   ATLANTIC BEACH
Jacob   Rockaway Beach
Riis
Park

                                    Atlantic Ocean

N

                        POI
                        Airport

0   10km
0   6 miles

wonder what the fuss is about. The subway is well policed by uniformed and plain-clothes officers. It is also a fact that the subway provides the quickest direct route between hundreds of points in Manhattan and the boroughs. And it is cheap. Take precautions. Stay with the crowd, avoid sparsely populated cars, do not display touristic naivety – for instance, do not peer at your map. Swot up your route in advance (for bus or subway information, *tel: (718) 330 1234*). Be alert. Do not keep your money, cheque book or credit cards where an opportunist can grab them. Wear your shoulder bag with the fastening against your body. Men should not strap-hang with their jackets gaping open revealing a wallet. It may be wise to use surface transport late at night. Just be as sensible as you would be in a similar situation at home.

The boys in blue – New York's cops lead the city's ongoing fight against crime

Bridges and tunnels

The East River separates Manhattan from Queens and Brooklyn. The Harlem River separates Manhattan from the Bronx. The Hudson River separates Manhattan from New Jersey which, although a different state, provides Manhattan with much of its workforce. Consequently, New York City has more than 60 bridges. Circle Line's 56km (35-mile) cruise around Manhattan Island passes under 20 of them and through 4 tunnels and 73 transit subways.

Recognising the snob appeal of Manhattan, residents have a tendency to demonstrate superiority to New Yorkers from the other boroughs, referring to them as Bridge and Tunnel people. The beauty of Brooklyn Bridge is universally admired. It spans the East River and was regarded as the Eighth Wonder of the World when it opened in 1883. It was

The George Washington Bridge

the world's first steel suspension bridge, hanging between two 82m (268ft) towers and supported by steel wire cables. The work, led by John Roebling and his son, took 15 years.

In 1964 the 1,298m (4,260ft) Verrazano-Narrows Bridge was completed – for a time the world's longest suspension bridge. It links Staten Island with Brooklyn, and is named after the Italian explorer Giovanni da Verrazano who, in 1524, was the first white man to see what later became New York.

Manhattan Bridge, which leads off Canal Street to cross the East River to Brooklyn, has a much-ornamented archway.

Tolls are payable on many of the bridges and tunnels. Charges for some are payable in one direction only. For example, there is a fee for a car crossing the Verrazano-Narrows Bridge westward from Brooklyn to Staten Island, but the journey in the opposite direction is free. Drivers of cars using the Midtown Tunnel or the Triborough Bridge, both of which link Long Island with Manhattan, must pay a toll in each direction.

Two tunnels and a bridge carry traffic over or under the Hudson River between New Jersey and Manhattan. The George Washington Bridge, opened in 1931 and transporting 14 lanes of traffic, goes into the north of the borough at West 178th Street, making a graceful and sweeping connection between the neighbouring states.

The Lincoln Tunnel enters Manhattan at Midtown. The Holland

The pedestrian walkway across Brooklyn Bridge provides a close-up view of this engineering marvel

Many New Yorkers prefer to commute by cab

Near Triborough Bridge, just north of Hell Gate Bridge, looking towards Ward Island and Randall's Island, the turbulence at the meeting of the East River, Long Island Sound and Harlem River is much in evidence.

Queensboro Bridge, opened in 1909, has a 2,134m (7,000ft) span. It goes over the East River from East 60th Street, Manhattan, to Crescent Street, Queens, crossing Roosevelt Island. Although Roosevelt Island is mainly residential, with little of interest to see, many people make the crossing on Roosevelt Island Aerial Tramway just for the fun of it. This is a horizontal cable car system, which goes between 60th Street at Second Avenue and the island, following the line of Queensboro Bridge. The journey takes less than four minutes, providing great views, and costs the same as a regular subway ride.

Tunnel goes into Lower Manhattan, emerging at the western end of Canal Street. With Manhattan Bridge (no toll) at Canal Street's eastern end, it provides a direct connection between New Jersey and Long Island. A toll is charged on each of these three links for cars travelling east to Manhattan. There is no toll for westbound traffic.

At Murray Hill, the Queens-Midtown Tunnel, with entrances between First and Second avenues around 38th

Visitors should take time to accustom themselves to the distinctive city layout

Queensboro Bridge

Street, goes under the East River to Queens.

The model of the five boroughs at Queens Museum in Flushing Meadow illustrates how dependent New York City is on its bridges and tunnels.

What makes New Yorkers tick?

Like most Americans, New Yorkers are extremely articulate. But on a superficial level, when making comments to strangers, for example, they tend to be monosyllabic, delivering one-liners, or making the odd wisecrack straight-faced. It may sound blunt, but do not read it as unfriendly. These are not over-effusive people. The USA is as close as you can get to a classless society. Those serving you may be tomorrow's tycoons, yesterday's recession-hit graduates or today's workforce making a career in the vital hospitality industry.

However, while New Yorkers may not be class-conscious, in so far as it does not matter to them how your father earned a living, you should observe the concept that money talks, and bet your bottom dollar they are listening.

Most people in New York have either a positive or negative attitude towards drink. The trouble is, you do not know which it is until you have a large dry gin in your hand. 'Time for cocktails. We deserve it,' they say, leading you to the bar. Once your guilty pick-me-up is delivered, they may put you down by ordering themselves a Perrier or tomato juice.

It is only a form of one-upmanship. Enjoy your drink, and consider yourself one up on them!

New York Harbor

The Staten Island Ferry provides a good view of New York Harbor, discovered in 1524 by Italian explorer Giovanni da Verrazano who sailed into the natural harbour within which nestled the islands that were to form New York City. It was the Dutch who first established a settlement in lower Manhattan, but the harbour was too valuable to be acquired peacefully. Skirmishes to win ownership continued until the British gained control in 1674.

Circle Line cruises operate from the harbour

Over the years, a virtual sea of humanity has crossed the harbour into the mainland. To the many Africans who encountered it, it was just a frightening, floating stop on an arduous nightmare journey. There was a slave market on Wall Street. To others, it was the gateway to opportunity. More than 17 million immigrants disembarked here, mainly from Europe, to be processed and accepted as new Americans. Some were attracted by the wide expanses of the hinterland, but many chose to settle in the city, endowing it with its characteristic mix of cultures.

Seeing the harbour from the water gives a different perspective – the

The Staten Island Ferry, the best free sightseeing trip in the world

The Verrazano-Narrows Bridge

dramatic view of the Statue of Liberty against the backdrop of the Manhattan skyline is truly memorable, and gives the few who arrive by sea an advantage over the masses who now arrive by air.

Airline passengers, however, do get a bird's-eye glimpse of the harbour, with its narrow bottleneck between the Atlantic Ocean and the almost landlocked haven into which the Hudson River flows after its 492km (306-mile) journey. The river occupies a deep underwater canyon that provides good deep-water facilities for ocean-going ships entering Manhattan.

Ferries go to Staten Island, Ellis Island and Liberty Island. Circle Line cruises and World Yacht Dining cruises, operated by New York Cruise Lines, provide an opportunity to view the city's spectacular skyline and some of its famous landmarks from the surrounding waterways. In the evening, the company runs Harbor Lights cruises.

Across the narrow mouth of the harbour is the elegant Verrazano-Narrows Bridge, linking Staten Island and Brooklyn. At 1,298m (4,260ft), it was the longest bridge in the world when it opened in 1964. The Hudson River is 1,219m (4,000ft) wide in its lower reaches, separating New York from New Jersey.

Among the sights seen by passengers on the 56km (35-mile) trip around Manhattan Island are the Financial District landmarks – the World Financial Center, the New Jersey Palisades and the George Washington Bridge.

Manhattan

More than 1½ million people live in Manhattan, which has evolved over the past 400 years and is continually changing. The island measures approximately 22km (13½ miles) long by 3.6km (2¼ miles) wide at the widest point – less than 1.6km (1 mile) at its narrowest. Apart from the great green rectangle which is Central Park, it is almost all covered in buildings and roads.

Nothing could be simpler than the geography of Manhattan. The borough is divided into three major districts: Lower, Midtown and Upper Manhattan. Lower Manhattan is the most southerly area, generally agreed to extend as far north as 23rd Street. Midtown goes up to Central Park, and everywhere else is Upper Manhattan. Movement across the city is 'uptown', 'downtown' or 'crosstown'. Anywhere north of a given location is uptown; downtown is to the south; and crosstown is east or west.

South of Houston Street the grid pattern falls to bits. This was the first area of Manhattan to be settled, so its streets tend to follow Old World customs, and have names rather than numbers.

Avenues run from First on the East River to Twelfth on the Hudson River. There are some inconsistencies. For example, Lexington, Park and Madison avenues run between Third and Fifth avenues. Fourth Avenue is a short stretch extending from the Bowery to East 14th Street. Sixth Avenue is officially known as the Avenue of the Americas. Broadway is the wild card, running straight from Bowling Green to East 10th Street where it suddenly kinks westwards to West 79th Street. In the Upper East Side, York Avenue runs between First Avenue and the East River. In the Lower East Side avenues A, B, C and D lie between First Avenue and Roosevelt Parkway.

Before you start to explore the borough, you may like to sample one or more ways of getting an introductory perspective on Manhattan. There are two useful and pleasurable ways of doing this. One is to take the three-hour, 56km (35-mile) Circle Line cruise around the island (*see p184*). The second option is to cross the East River to Queens. In Flushing Meadow/Corona Park is the Queens Museum of Art (*www.queensmuseum.org*), which contains a constantly updated model of the five boroughs.

(*Cont. on p34*)

Lower Manhattan

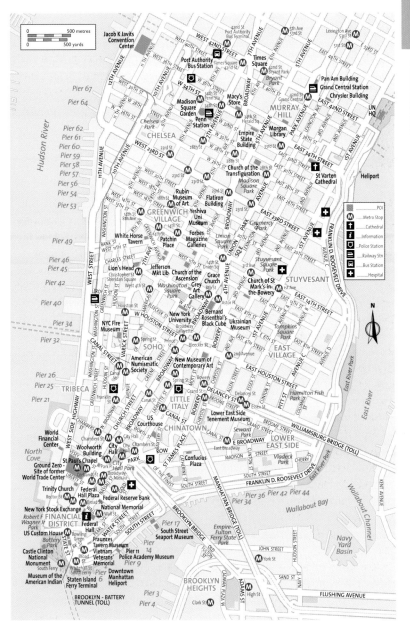

Walk: Battery Park – Financial District

New York's Financial District is at the southerly tip of Manhattan Island.

Allow 2 hours.

Begin from Staten Island Ferry Terminal (South Ferry subway station) and head west into Battery Park (see p34), staying close to the water's edge.

1 Battery Park

This park has lots of statuary and welcome greenery. The steps of the Atlantic Coast Memorial, a monument commemorating US servicemen who died in World War II, offer a splendid view of New York Harbor, including the Statue of Liberty.

A little further on is a statue of Giovanni da Verrazano, who sailed into New York Harbor in 1524. Also in the Park is Castle Clinton (*see p34*), a circular, brick-built fortress that was on an island 61m (200ft) offshore when it was built in 1811.

From Castle Clinton walk inland along the broad mall, passing the Netherlands Memorial commemorating the exchange of beads that purchased Manhattan from the Indians in 1626, and leave the park at State St.

2 Bowling Green

On the opposite side of State Street is the ornate US Custom House, built in 1907 on the site of the old Fort Amsterdam, now the Museum of the American Indian. Statuary symbolising the various continents was sculpted by Daniel Chester French, who created President Abraham Lincoln's statue at the Lincoln Memorial in Washington, DC. The Custom House stands opposite Bowling Green, opened in 1773 as New York's first public park. The statue of Britain's King George III here was toppled and melted down for bullets soon after the American Declaration of Independence in July 1776.

Head south (right) along State St, passing the shrine of St Elizabeth Ann Seton, the first American-born saint. Turn left at Whitehall St, right into Water St, then left at Broad St.

3 Broad Street

This is where New York's past and present converge. Interspersed among the glitz of modern commerce are pre-Independence relics. At Pearl and Broad streets is Fraunces Tavern Museum (*see p39*), a three-storey Georgian brick building where George Washington bade his troops farewell in 1783. The course of the old Stone Street, built by the Dutch, is marked by a line of paving stones in the lobby of a modern office complex at 85 Broad Street. *From Pearl St head away from Broad St to reach Hanover Square.*

4 Hanover Square

The first printing press in the American colonies was established here, and Captain Kidd was once a resident. India House, former site of the New York Cotton Exchange, now houses the classic bar, Harry's of Hanover Square. To the west of Hanover Square is Delmonico's restaurant, originally opened in 1827.

Continue up William St, turn left into Wall St.

5 Wall Street

The golden gulch, Wall Street (*see pp32–3*) cleaves through the skyscrapers for 0.5km (¹/₃ mile). Wall Street follows the line of a wooden wall built by the Dutch to keep the Native Americans and British trade rivals at bay. A statue of George Washington on the steps of the Federal Hall National Memorial marks the spot where the first US president was sworn in. The New York Stock Exchange holds a prominent position. Trinity Church (*see p57*), once the city's tallest building, dates from 1846. It is the third church on the site; its charter goes back to 1697.

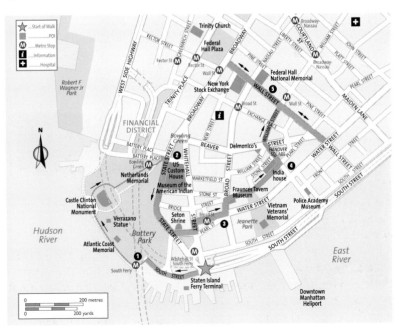

Wall Street

When most visitors think of the rich and powerful of New York – and, indeed, the world's business community – a tableau of Wall Street comes to mind. Long known as the epicentre of New York's Financial District, that's not actually an accurate depiction anymore. Even the iconic *Charging Bull* sculpture by Arturo Di Modica, signifying the important bull market economy, is no longer located on Wall Street; instead, it can be found nearby in Bowling Green. Many things about Wall Street have changed in recent years.

The shift began even before 11 September, when technology outpaced tradition and computer transactions eliminated many of the jobs on the trading floor of the New York Stock Exchange. After 9/11, a mass exodus of financial companies out of the area meant the power centre became decentralised, with

Fortunes are won and lost in Wall Street's financial institutions

The impressive façade of the New York Stock Exchange

important financial leaders now located uptown on Park Avenue or even in neighbouring states of Connecticut and New Jersey.

The biggest changes came to Wall Street in 2008 when the United States experienced a financial meltdown that triggered repercussions all over the world. Troubling news emerged, including a failed housing market due to the high default rate of subprime and adjustable rate mortgages, the bankruptcy of financial services company Lehman Brothers and the collapse and subsequent sale of Bear Stearns investment bank to JPMorgan Chase.

To add insult to injury, 2009 saw supposed investment guru Bernie Madoff plead guilty to stealing billions of dollars from investors via a Ponzi scheme. With news like that, Main Street added Wall Street to its list of *personae non gratae*. It will take a long time for Wall Street to build back up its financial portfolio as well as the trust of the American people.

Still, the area – with its skyscrapers commingling with architecture of the Gilded Art – is certainly worth visiting. Don't miss these buildings: Federal Hall, the Bankers Trust Company Building/14 Wall Street and the New York Stock Exchange.

LOWER MANHATTAN
American Numismatic Society
Coins, medals and decorations from many countries are displayed.
75 Varick St at Canal St. Tel: (212) 571 4470; www.numismatics.org. Open: Mon–Fri 9.30am–4.30pm. Free admission. Subway: Canal Street Station.

Battery Park
This green esplanade overlooks New York Harbor, Staten Island, Liberty Island and Governor's Island. Established in 1870 from 9ha (22 acres) of landfill, it is named after the battery of cannons lined around the shore (*see p30*).
Lower Manhattan. Subway: Bowling Green.

Brooklyn Bridge
One of the great engineering feats of the 19th century, and the first suspension bridge made of steel cables, it is still considered by many to be the most beautiful bridge in the world. Before it opened in 1883, the only way across the East River was by ferry. The view of Manhattan from the pedestrian walkway is spectacular, especially at night.
Lower Manhattan. Subway: Brooklyn Bridge/City Hall.

Castle Clinton National Monument
The fort was built to defend New York Harbor during the war of 1812. It became an entertainment centre called Castle Garden in 1824, then an immigration depot. About 8 million people entered the USA through Castle Clinton between 1855 and 1890. Later it became a popular aquarium.

It was given national monument status in 1946, and now contains a museum depicting its past. Tickets for the Statue of Liberty Ferry are sold nearby.
Battery Park. Tel: (212) 344 7220; www.nps.gov/cacl. Open: daily 8.30am–5pm. Closed Christmas Day. Free admission. Subway: Bowling Green.

Church of the Transfiguration
Chinese Catholics worship here in what was once the Zion Episcopal Church. It dates from 1801, long before the arrival of the Chinese.
Mott St & Park St, Chinatown.

City Hall
The seat of New York's municipal government since 1811, this is an outstanding example of Federal period architecture. This is a landmark building which some have described as the most beautiful in the USA. It is elegant from its frontal columns to its cupola, topped with a figure of Lady Justice. The mayor's office is on the ground floor. What used to be the governor's office has become a museum and portrait gallery.
City Hall Park, Broadway/Murray St. Tel: (212) 788 3000; www.nyc.gov; Tel: (tours) (212) 788 2170. Tours free on weekdays but reservations required. Subway: City Hall/Broadway.

Ellis Island National Monument

Ellis Island is one of 40 islands around New York. Visitors to the **Ellis Island Immigration Museum** (*see p38*), opened in 1990, will not find it difficult to visualise the scene when immigrants, mainly from Europe, arrived on American soil after long, crowded and often arduous voyages. Many feared desperately that they would be turned back for health or other reasons. However, 17 million new Americans were 'processed' – each took about four hours – and were allowed entry between 1892 and 1954.

Close your eyes in the museum and you can imagine shuffling along in a seemingly never-ending line of weary hopefuls, pausing for medical checks, for the scrutinising of documents, and for questions, questions, questions in an alien tongue, voices reverberating off the thick walls. Most had reached their promised land, and would be admitted to form ethnic neighbourhoods in New York, or to put down roots elsewhere in the USA. Others, about 10 per cent, were unacceptable, and ordered to be dispatched home. Some could not face this and quietly committed suicide – up to half a dozen a month, some 3,000 in all. Some of those who were rejected flung themselves from the deck of the ship carrying them homeward, hoping to swim across to Manhattan's shore, and perished in the attempt.

Even from the shore, Ellis Island evokes an atmosphere of foreboding, its dark brick buildings reminiscent

(*Cont. on p38*)

Manhattan

The elegant façade of City Hall

Walk: Chinatown

Settled by 20th-century immigrants from China, this is a vibrant enclave. It's easy to be sidetracked as restaurants, coffee houses, Buddhist temples and bazaars command attention.

Allow 1½ hours.

Begin at the junction of Bowery and Canal St (nearest subway station is Grand St, two blocks north). Notice the dome of the old Police Headquarters to the right, behind you. Turn south down Bowery.

1 Bowery

Not Manhattan's most salubrious thoroughfare, Bowery was once the scene of popular musical and theatrical entertainment. Today, all this has gone, and down-and-outs live rough on the street. Confucius Plaza at 19 Bowery has a statue of the Chinese philosopher in front of a modern residential development. On the corner of Pell Street, at 18 Bowery, is Edward Mooney House, the oldest known town house surviving in Manhattan. Built about 1789, it was originally the home of a wealthy meat merchant who bred racehorses. In modern times it has been, among other things, a betting parlour.

Continue south along Bowery to Chatham Square.

2 Chatham Square

This lies at the intersection of ten streets, and is as much a hazard for pedestrians as it is for motor traffic. Chinese victims of American wars are honoured by a memorial arch in the centre of the square. On the east side at East Broadway is a pagoda-style building housing a bank.

At the southwest corner of Chatham Square turn into Worth St, then right into Mulberry St.

3 Mulberry Street

On the left you will see Columbus Park, formerly an immigrant slum area. Mulberry Street extends north into Little Italy. Canal Street once marked the boundary between Little Italy and Chinatown, but Asians have gradually spread into the area.

Turn right into Park St, then left into Mott St.

A lively, bustling enclave

4 Mott Street

Dominating the corner of Mott and Park streets is the imposing Church of the Transfiguration, built early in the 19th century, where the Chinese Catholics worship. It was originally the Zion Episcopal Church. At No 8 Mott Street is the Chinatown Fair amusement arcade. Mott Street, the lively, teeming heart of New York's Chinatown, is the place to buy bargain kitchenware, chopsticks and woks, as well as Mandarin, Shanghai, Cantonese and other Far Eastern cuisines. Ingredients for many Asian dishes can also be found here and there are good selections of Eastern souvenirs, such as jade ornaments and silks. Take a look along narrow Pell Street and Doyers Street, which lead off it. The corner of these streets used to be called 'The Bloody Angle' – bodies of men killed in the Tong (clan association) Wars were often dumped here. On the brighter side, this area is where revelries are focused during the Chinese New Year, celebrated at the first full moon after 19 January. Traditional Chinese

dragons parade through the streets, firework displays ward off evil spirits and martial arts are deftly demonstrated.

Return to Mott St. Turn right, then left at Bayard St, right into Mulberry St and right into Canal St.

5 Canal Street

Like Bayard Street, Canal Street has food stalls piled high with herbs, Chinese mushrooms, bean curd, snow peas, dried fungi, fresh seafood and exotic fruit and vegetables. There are also clothing discount stores, shops selling electrical goods and the enticing Kam Man supermarket. Originally a drainage waterway, from which it took its name, Canal Street links the Holland Tunnel in the west with Manhattan Bridge in the east, and provides a continuous connection between New Jersey and Long Island. The Museum of Chinese in the Americas is nearby on Centre Street. A short walk eastwards takes you back to Confucius Plaza.

Continue a few metres along Canal St for a view to the right of the Manhattan Bridge, with its central triumphal arch.

of a 19th-century workhouse. But it also generates a strong sense of not-so-distant history. Two in five Americans won US citizenship via Ellis Island in the early days, and for their descendants, as well as for overseas visitors today, the resurrected immigration station is a deeply thought-provoking experience.

Ellis Island Immigration Museum

This museum traces the history of immigration to America. Statue Cruises has daily departures from the South Ferry at Battery Park.
Tel: (212) 363 3200; www.nps.gov.
Ferry departures: daily 9.30am–5.15pm.
Free admission with ferry ticket.
Subway: Bowling St.

Federal Hall National Memorial

A Doric temple-style building erected in 1842 on the site of Washington's inauguration as first President of the USA on 30 April 1789. It contains a museum of New York's Colonial and early Federal periods with exhibits, films and 18th-century folk music.
26 Wall St/Nassau St.
Tel: (212) 825 6888; www.nps.gov.
Open: Mon–Fri 9am–5pm.
Free admission. Subway: Broad St/Wall St.

Once filled with anxious immigrants, this stately building is now the Ellis Island Immigration Museum

Federal Reserve Bank of New York

A bank for banks, with more gold stored in its subterranean vaults than in Fort Knox. The imposing building is modelled on the Strozzi Palace in Florence. The wealth of nations is locked away in private chambers, shifting from nation to nation in a short move from one chamber to another.
33 Liberty St. Tel: (212) 720 6130; www.newyorkfed.org. Free guided tour by appointment, Mon–Fri; several daily. Subway: Wall St/William St.

Forbes Magazine Galleries

Permanent exhibition of the late publisher Malcolm Forbes's collection of 500 toy boats, 12,000 toy soldiers and the world's largest clutch of Fabergé eggs. There are changing exhibitions of paintings.
60 5th Ave. Tel: (212) 206 5548; www.forbesgalleries.com. Open: Tue–Sat 10am–4pm. Free admission. Subway: Union Square.

Fraunces Tavern Museum

Five historic buildings, including the restored 18th-century tavern where, in the Long Room, Washington bade farewell to his officers celebrating the British leaving New York after the Revolutionary War in 1783. The restaurant has existed for more than 200 years. There is a bar room and a gift shop. The museum has decorative arts, paintings, prints, manuscripts, period rooms, 18th- and 19th-century memorabilia – including Washington's teeth and hair – and changing exhibitions.
54 Pearl St/Broad St. Tel: (212) 425 1778; www.frauncestavernmuseum.org. Open: Mon–Sat noon–5pm. Admission charge. Subway: Whitehall St/South Ferry.

Greenwich Village

Oddly enough, Greenwich Village does not have much in the way of formal sights – museums, churches and the like – but the character of its streets varies from the picturesque to the eccentric. The best thing is to wander, look and flop on to a bar stool or café chair now and then to reflect on what you have seen. There will have been plenty in this engaging and stimulating community.

Bedford Street

One of the quietest and most desirable of Village streets. Among its quaint houses is No 75½, just over 2.7m (9ft) wide, and New York's narrowest dwelling. The clapboard house next door was built in 1799 and is said to be the oldest in the Village. At No 80 is Chumleys, a speakeasy during the Prohibition days, but now a cosy bar and restaurant. James Joyce finished writing *Ulysses* at one of its tables.
Subway: Christopher St/Sheridan Square. Bus: M13.

Walk: East Village

Highly fashionable in the 19th century, when it was the home of the wealthy, East Village later became a more workaday place for several decades. In the 1950s it attracted the beatniks. Now it has been regentrified.

Allow 1 hour.

Begin at the Astor Place subway station. Head east along Stuyvesant St.

1 Stuyvesant Street

The land here was once part of the Dutch governor Peter Stuyvesant's farm or *bouwerie*, from which the nearby thoroughfare got its name. There are some fine 19th-century houses, including No 21, built in 1804 as a wedding gift for his great-great-granddaughter. At the end of the street is the Church of St Mark's-in-the-Bowery (*see p52*), on the site of the mansion where Stuyvesant lived. Since 1920 it has been a centre for avant-garde cultural activity as well as worship.
Turn right along 2nd Ave.

2 Second Avenue

The street was a thriving ethnic theatre district in the early 1900s. Stars set into the sidewalk pay tribute to Yiddish performers of that time.
Continue to St Mark's Place.

3 St Mark's Place

St Mark's Place was the centre of the Beat Generation when Allen Ginsberg, Jack Kerouac and other 1950s writers lived here. An earlier resident – at No 77 – was the British-born poet W H Auden. Between Second and Third avenues, St Mark's Place has offbeat stores, vegetarian restaurants, stalls and boutiques. At St Mark's Bookshop (No 12) you can spend time among the volumes and find out about local events from the bulletin board.
Turn right into St Mark's Place and left on to 3rd Ave to E 7th St.

4 East 7th Street

At No 15 is McSorley's Old Ale House, opened in 1854, and a haunt of Brendan Behan, the Irish dramatist. Nearby, the Ukrainian Shop and St George's Ukrainian Catholic Church reflect a thriving ethnic community.
Continue along 3rd Ave to Cooper Square.

5 Cooper Square

The square is dominated by the Cooper Union Foundation Building, founded in 1859 by Peter Cooper as a non fee-paying college for working-class students. His statue stands in the square. Public speakers were invited to use the Great Hall of the college of art, architecture and engineering, among them Abraham Lincoln, who attacked slavery in an electioneering address. *Walk north along 4th Ave, turning left into Astor Place.*

6 Astor Place

Two traffic islands on the junction are spectacularly ornamented. A cast-iron sculpture marks a subway entrance, and the vast rotating black cube, *Alamo*, is by Bernard Rosenthal. *Turn left into Lafayette St.*

7 Lafayette Street

On the right, Colonnade Row has four houses dating from 1833, once occupied by the millionaires Astor and Vanderbilt.

Across the road at No 425 is the Public Theater, in Italian Renaissance style. It was originally opened by Astor in 1854 as New York's first free library. One of the earliest venues for Off-Broadway productions, it was founded by Joseph Papp in 1954 and opened in the late 1960s with the rock musical *Hair*. The theatre has also been involved in a Shakespeare Marathon, with the object of performing each of the Bard's works over a six-year period. *Continue down Lafayette St, turning right into Bleecker St.*

8 Bleecker Street

Number 65 is the 1898 Bayard Building, the only New York structure that was designed by the famous Chicago skyscraper architect Louis Sullivan. *Return to Lafayette St for the Bleecker St subway station.*

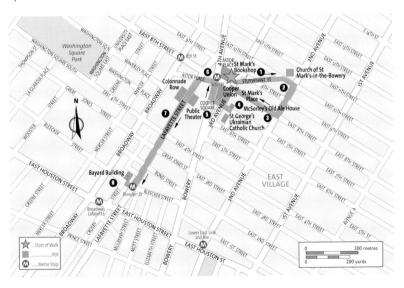

Village life

Charming house fronts in Washington Square

The concept of 'village' life in a place as urban and urbane as New York may seem curious, if not downright pretentious. But two parts of the city not only carry the word 'village' as part of their name, but also are totally different from the rest in tempo and character.

Greenwich Village, which some residents of Manhattan dismiss these days as passé, continues to be what it has always been: a community apart. Although there is no longer a recognisable literati, there is an air of successful creativity among its elegant homes and quaint streets that are sandwiched between the Hudson River to the west and Broadway to the east with 14th Street guarding its upper boundary and Houston Street marking off the southern border. Would-be writers gather at the Figaro and other sidewalk cafés, poring over the pages of *Village Voice* and putting the world to rights, though the attitudes they strike are less iconoclastic than those of the hell-raising Beat Generation writers who preceded them in the 1950s. Gay bars on Christopher Street and events like Halloween, when strangely costumed crowds parade uninhibitedly through the streets, prove that Greenwich Village still attracts the unconventional and bohemian, if not the downright eccentric.

So does neighbouring East Village, on the other side of Broadway, where 8th Street becomes St Mark's Place, a bizarre bazaar of alternative-living stalls, stores and restaurants. The area has always attracted offbeat writers and artists and revolutionary thinkers. This was where Edward Albee (*Who's Afraid of Virginia Woolf?*), Theodore

Café life in the Village

Dreiser and e e cummings lived, where the author of *Moby Dick*, Herman Melville, worked as a customs inspector when he was unable to earn his living as a writer, and where he began *Billy Budd*, his last novel. George Gershwin gave his first public recital here, and the Astors and Vanderbilts initially lived here. This was where Jack Kerouac, Allen Ginsberg and other Beat Generation figures lived it up; avant-garde theatre thrives here yet. Gentrification is putting a new shine on East Village, but it, too, will always be just that little bit different.

Rising costs of housing have all but pushed out most 'starving artists' from both Greenwich Village and the East Village. Creative types are now much more likely to make their home in Williamsburg, Brooklyn.

Bleecker Street, Sixth Avenue

The lively heart of Greenwich Village. The area around the intersection has lots of shops, bars and sidewalk cafés, and is a meeting place for New York University students and others in the young set. The Café Figaro and others nearby were where the Beat writers got together in the 1950s (*see pp42–3*).
Subway: Christopher St/Sheridan Square. Bus: M5 & M6.

Christopher Street

Running from West Street, fronting the Hudson River, to Sheridan Square, the street is the focal point for the Village's gay community.
Subway: Christopher St/Sheridan Square. Bus: M13.

Church of the Ascension

A small, Gothic-style brownstone church designed by Richard Upjohn, architect of Trinity Church in the Financial District. Special features are its stained-glass windows by John La Farge and its marble altar sculpture.
12 W 11th St/5th Ave. Tel: (212) 254 8620; www.ascensionnyc.org. Subway: Broadway/W 8th St. Bus: M2, M3 & M5.

Grey Art Gallery

Part of the art department of New York University, with a permanent collection of post-1940s American works. In addition, contemporary art is featured in the many changing exhibitions held here.

100 Washington Square East. Tel: (212) 998 6780; www.nyu.edu/greyart. Open: Tue, Thur & Fri 11am–6pm, Wed 11am–8pm, Sat 11am–5pm. Donation suggested. Subway: Broadway/W 8th St. Bus: M2, M3 & M13.

Jefferson Market Courthouse

Built as a courthouse in 1876, the building is now used as a branch of the New York Public Library. Because of its alternating bands of red brick and granite, locals describe the building as being in the Lean Bacon style of architecture. It is, in fact, Victorian Gothic, and one of its architects was Calvert Vaux, of Central Park fame.
425 6th Ave. Subway: Christopher St/Sheridan Square. Bus: M5 & M6.

The Lion's Head

Site of the famous literary bar where writers like Norman Mailer and Frank McCourt used to hang out.
59 Christopher St, opposite Christopher Park with statue of Civil War general Philip Sheridan. Subway: Christopher St/Sheridan Square. Bus: M13.

Patchin Place

A courtyard of neat mews cottages which have been home at various times to such literary figures as John Masefield, Theodore Dreiser, Eugene O'Neill and e e cummings.
W 10th St, just west of 6th Ave.

Subway: Christopher St/Sheridan Square. Bus: M5 & M6.

Washington Square

Chess players, rollerskaters, street entertainers, art shows – hardly the Washington Square novelist Henry James wrote about in his novel of that name, but still the nominal centre of Greenwich Village. It is dominated by the triumphal arch commemorating the centenary of George Washington's inauguration as president. Most of the surrounding buildings belong to New York University.
Subway: W 10th St/Washington Square. Bus: M5 & M6.

The White Horse Tavern

An inexpensive bar with literary connections dating to the late 1880s. This is the one in which Welsh poet Dylan Thomas, author of *Under Milk Wood* and a prodigious drinker, drank his last. Academics still gather here, especially in the outdoor café open in warm weather.
567 Hudson St. Tel: (212) 989 3956. Subway: Christopher St/Sheridan Square. Bus: M10.

Lower East Side Tenement Museum

America's first urban living history museum, interpreting immigrant history. Allows only guided tours. Historic walking tours are offered in the discount shopping district.
97 Orchard St (Delancy/Broome sts). Tel: (212) 431 0233; www.tenement.org. Guided tours: daily from 10.30am.

Admission charge. Subway: Delancy St/Essex St.

Museum of the American Indian

Devoted to the cultures of the North, Central and South American Indian. This is the largest collection of Native American artefacts in the USA, and includes possessions of Sitting Bull and Geronimo.
1 Bowling Green (State/Whitehall sts). Tel: (212) 514 3700; www.nmai.si.edu. Open: Fri–Wed 10am–5pm, Thur 10am–8pm. Museum shop open: 10am–5pm. Free admission. Subway: Bowling Green.

New Museum of Contemporary Art

Devoted solely to the art and ideas of our time, this museum explores offbeat issues, and features changing exhibitions of international artists' work.
235 Bowery/Prince St. Tel: (212) 219 1222; www.newmuseum.org. Open: Wed noon–6pm, Thur & Fri noon–9pm, Sat & Sun noon–6pm. Admission charge. Subway: Spring St or Prince St.

New York City Fire Museum

Collections of the city Fire Department and Home Insurance Company and a history of fire-fighting in the city, situated in a 1904 firehouse.
278 Spring St (Hudson/Varick sts). Tel: (212) 691 1303; www.nycfiremuseum.org.

(*Cont. on p48*)

Walk: Greenwich Village

Greenwich Village manages to retain a hint of a rural atmosphere – there were still farms here in the 19th century. Some of its winding streets are former cattle trails and country lanes.

Allow 2 hours.

Begin at Washington Square at the south end of 5th Ave (subway station at West 4th St/Washington Square). Proceed clockwise round the square.

1 Washington Square

Washington Arch, designed by Stanford White to commemorate the centenary of the inauguration of the first US president, was first built in wood and later, in 1895, in stone. Most buildings around the square are part of New York University. The oldest, 20 Washington Square North, dates from before 1830.

The Grey Art Gallery, in the university's main building, exhibits mainly contemporary art. The Loeb Students' Center stands on the site of The House of Genius, which has housed writers such as Theodore Dreiser, O Henry and Eugene O'Neill.

At the square's southwest corner, turn left into MacDougal St.

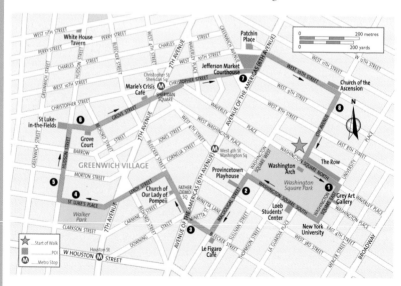

2 MacDougal Street

Numbers 130 and 132 were the home of Louisa M Alcott, who wrote *Little Women* there. The nearby Provincetown Playhouse staged premiere performances of Eugene O'Neill's plays.
Continue along MacDougal St to Bleecker St and turn right.

3 Bleecker Street

Bleecker Street's junction with MacDougal Street and Sixth Avenue has sidewalk cafés popularised by literary figures in the 1950s. On the opposite side of Sixth Avenue at Carmine Street is the Church of Our Lady of Pompeii.
Cross 6th Ave. Continue along Bleecker St, turning left into Leroy St. Cross 7th Ave to enter St Luke's Place.

4 St Luke's Place

This row of elegant mid-19th-century brownstone houses includes the house (No 16) in which novelist Theodore Dreiser wrote *An American Tragedy*.
Turn right into Hudson St.

5 Hudson Street

The Church of St Luke-in-the-Fields stood by the river bank when it was built in 1821.
Turn right down Grove St.

6 Grove Street

Grove Street and parallel Christopher Street form New York's best-known gay area. Marie's Crisis Café was the former home of Thomas Paine, author of *The Rights of Man*. An iron gate on Grove Street marks Grove Court.
Cross Sheridan Square into Christopher St and continue to 6th Ave.

7 Avenue of the Americas (Sixth Avenue)

In the triangle formed by Sixth Avenue, Greenwich Avenue and West 10th Street is located the former Jefferson Market Courthouse dating from 1876.
Cross 6th Ave and take W 10th St to 5th Ave.

8 Fifth Avenue

On the corner of West 10th Street and Fifth Avenue, the 1840 Church of the Ascension has stained-glass windows, and an altar mural by John La Farge.
Turn right on to 5th Ave and return to Washington Arch.

Washington Square was the setting for Henry James's novel of love and betrayal

Walk: Greenwich Village

Open: Tue–Sat 10am–5pm, Sun 10am–4pm. Donation suggested. Subway: Spring St.

New York Stock Exchange

Located on Wall Street, here is one of the largest and busiest stock exchanges in the world. The Greek Revival façade is the most famous symbol of American finance. Not open to the public.
Subway: Broad St/Wall St.

Police Academy Museum

Night sticks and old uniforms in a huge collection of memorabilia of the NYPD.
100 Old Slip/Front St. Tel: (212) 480 3100; www.nycpolicemuseum.org. Open: Mon–Sat 10am–5pm. Admission charge. Subway: Wall St.

Rubin Museum of Art

The Rubin focuses on Himalayan art and its preservation.
150 W 17th St/7th Ave. Tel: (212) 620 5000; www.rmanyc.org. Open: Sat & Sun 11am–6pm, Mon & Thur 11am–5pm, Wed 11am–7pm, Fri 11am–10pm. Admission charge. Subway: 18th St at 7th Ave.

South Street Seaport Museum

Long gone are the days when New York's busy Seaport at South Street saw cargo ships sailing off to distant lands. The port's heyday was in the first half of the 19th century, the golden age of sail, when a forest of tall masts lined the East River. It was in the 1860s that trade moved away – some of it to the other

side of Manhattan Island, where the deeper water of the Hudson River suited the new steamships. (*See also Walk pp54–5.*)

South Street went further into decline, its warehouses crumbling, with only the fishing industry and a handful of chandleries continuing in business.

Today, the area has been revitalised as a nautical museum without walls. The 11-block cobblestoned pedestrian-only South Street Seaport Historic District buzzes with activity. Seafood restaurants, shops, bars, piers, craft centres, galleries and museums draw New Yorkers and visitors alike. Ships of 100 years ago can be visited, and harbour trips enjoyed. In summer, free street entertainment is provided by jugglers, puppeteers, mime artists, jazz groups and other musicians.

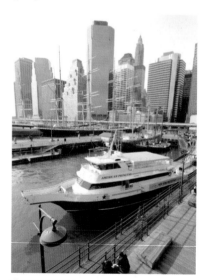

The Seaport area

The Seaport complex has been completely renovated

All this has happened since the 1960s, with most of the restored area opening to the public in 1983. The development has been one of the city's great commercial successes.

Giving the area added historical significance was the Fulton Fish Market, which had been in business since 1822. It used to open from midnight until 8am, and dawn would see local restaurant owners bidding for the best catches. Then in 2005 the fish market was moved to hygienic new premises in the Bronx, taking with it a big part of the Seaport's history and atmosphere.

The restored red-brick warehouses, which form Schermerhorn Row, date from 1811, and are considered the Seaport's architectural *pièce de résistance*. The buildings, from Nos 2–18 Fulton Street, 189–195 Front Street and 91–92 South Street, now contain a variety of novelty shops, restaurants and cafés, and the Seaport Museum Visitors' Center.

All 18 museums at South Street Seaport are housed in renovated buildings. The museum block is on Water Street between Fulton and Beekman streets, where the Seaport Gallery can be found.

More shops, restaurants and speciality food stores are in the three-storey Fulton Market Building bounded by South, Fulton, Front and Beekman streets. It was built in 1983 to harmonise with restored properties.

A children's centre offers workshops and holiday programmes. At the Maritime Crafts Center, specialists carve intricate wooden figureheads and work on model ships.

(*Cont. on p52*)

Walk: SoHo

Barely 30 years ago, SoHo (SOuth of HOuston Street) was described as a commercial slum, and there was a strong move to tear the place down. It was saved by the efforts of preservationists and a powerful artistic lobby.

Allow 1 hour.

Begin at Broadway/Lafayette subway station. Head south on Broadway.

1 Broadway

The area's artistic flavour is evident in the number of art galleries in the neighbourhood. Just beyond Prince Street is the 1904 'Little' Singer Building, whose cast-iron construction and innovative wide windows set the style for the architecture of the 1950s. Food, presented as an art form, can be seen at the upmarket Dean and DeLuca store across the street. At the northeast corner of Broome Street and Broadway

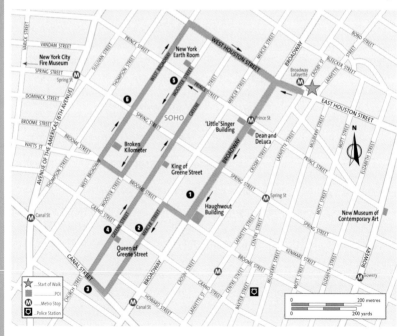

is the 'cast-iron palazzo' – the Haughwout Building. Built in 1857 and inspired by the architecture of Venice, this is where Elisha Otis installed his first practical passenger elevator.
Turn right into Broome St, then left into Mercer St.

2 Mercer Street

Evidence of the street's resident industry can be found in the fabric remnants thrown out from upstairs garment workshops.
Continue to the end of Mercer St, turning right into Canal St.

3 Canal Street

This is the frontier between SoHo and TriBeCa, a vibrant thoroughfare with a market atmosphere.
Turn right into Greene St.

4 Greene Street

This boasts the city's longest stretch of cast-iron buildings, between Canal and Grand streets. The building at Nos 28–30 is known as the Queen of Greene Street. Built in 1873, it has many of the decorative features which became possible when this new construction method was introduced in the 19th century. The King of Greene Street, at Nos 72–76, is a splendid Renaissance-style building and today houses art galleries and an upmarket antiques shop. On the southwest corner of Prince and Greene streets, the architectural features usually found only on the front of a cast-iron building appear to be continued along the side. But it is only an illusion: a mural painted in 1973 by the artist Richard Haas.
Turn left on to Prince St, then right into Wooster St.

5 Wooster Street

Wooster Street is one of the few SoHo thoroughfares still surfaced with the smooth, Belgian-style stone blocks that replaced the earlier cobblestones. At 141 Wooster Street is the *New York Earth Room*, a sculpture in soil by Walter de Maria. The *Earth Room* is a permanent exhibit maintained by the non-profit Dia Art Foundation, which also features temporary shows at 77 Wooster Street.
Return south along Wooster St, turn right into Broome St, then right again on West Broadway.

6 West Broadway

West Broadway is unquestionably SoHo's beating heart. At 393 West Broadway is another Dia Art Foundation exhibit of a work by Walter de Maria (the *Broken Kilometer*).
Continue up West Broadway, turn right into West Houston St; end the walk back at Broadway/Lafayette subway station.

An intriguing façade in SoHo

The galleries, ships and restored commercial district which form South Street Seaport Museum, from Water Street to South Street, are open daily throughout the year.

Eight historic ships can be visited at Piers 15 and 16. The Ambrose is a small scarlet lightship, which once guided steamers into the Port of New York. The *Wavertree* is a three-masted tall ship more than a century old. The *W O Decker* is a wooden tugboat dating from 1930, and the *Lettie G Howard* is the last Gloucester fishing schooner.
12 Fulton St.
Tel: (212) 748 8600;
www.southstreetseaportmuseum.org.
Open: daily 10am–5pm. Subway: Fulton, William St.

Church of St Mark's-in-the-Bowery

This church dates from 1799 and is built on the site of Peter Stuyvesant's farm (*see p40*). The Greek Revival steeple was added in 1826, and the cast-iron portico in 1858. Further restoration was carried out after the fire of 1978. The church is old in years, but young in outlook. Pews have been removed to allow dancers, poets and performing artists to entertain.
East Village at 2nd Ave/10th St.

St Paul's Chapel

Said to be the oldest public building in Manhattan in continuous use since its completion in 1766. This national landmark is where George Washington

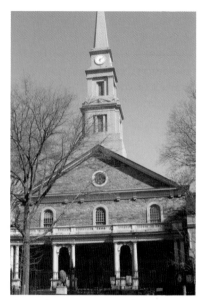
Church of St Mark's-in-the-Bowery

worshipped, and his pew is one of the things everyone goes to see. Tours of the chapel with its pastel blue and pink interior are by appointment.
Broadway at Fulton & Vesey sts.
Tel: (212) 233 4164;
www.trinitywallstreet.org. Open: Mon–Fri 10am–6pm, Sat 10am–4pm, Sun 7am–3pm. Subway: Fulton St/Broadway.

Statue of Liberty

Liberty Enlightening the World, better known as the Statue of Liberty, a national monument, is as popular today as she ever was, a universal symbol of democratic freedom. Her size is impressive. She stands 46m (152ft) tall on her 27m (89ft) pedestal, and measures 10.7m (420in) around the waist. Her unsmiling mouth is 1m (3ft) wide.

Officially, Liberty Island is in New Jersey waters, but the statue has been adjudged to be in New York State, and has a New York City post office address.

The 5.5ha (13½-acre) site of the statue has been called Liberty Island since 1956. Originally called Oyster Island, it became Love Island in 1670. In the Revolutionary War it was named Kennedy's Island, and in 1841, when a fort was built on it, it became Fort Wood. The star-shaped wall around the base is part of the former US Fort Wood, and formed part of the defences of New York City between 1841 and 1877. It has also been called Bedloe's Island after Isaac Bedloe, to whom it had once been granted.

In 1986 the statue, which was declared a national monument by President Calvin Coolidge in 1924, underwent a much-needed restoration programme. She had stood for 100 years, and had begun her existence 12 years before that when the French sculptor Frédéric Auguste Bartholdi started to interpret the design of Alexandre Gustave Eiffel, of Eiffel Tower fame.

The French writer Edouard de Laboulaye is credited with having the idea of the statue at the time of the USA centennial in 1876. He felt that the 1778 alliance between France and the USA should be suitably commemorated. Eiffel duly got busy at his drawing board, designing a skeleton of iron, and Bartholdi put on

(*Cont. on p56*)

Crossing the harbour by ferry provides the perfect opportunity to photograph the Statue of Liberty

Walk: St Paul's Chapel – South Street Seaport

This part of Lower Manhattan starts where the World Trade Center once stood and includes the Woolworth Building, the courts and the restored waterfront on the East River.

Allow 2 hours.

Begin on Church St. Head northwards and turn right on Fulton St and then left to reach Broadway.

1 Broadway

St Paul's Chapel, on the corner of Broadway and Fulton Street, dates from 1766 and is Manhattan's oldest surviving church (*see p52*). Modelled after St Martin-in-the-Fields, London, St Paul's was where George Washington worshipped, and where he prayed after his inauguration as president. At Park Place and Broadway is the 241m (792ft) Woolworth Building. This was the world's tallest building when it opened in 1913 as the headquarters of the Woolworth empire. It was designed by prominent American architect Cass Gilbert. Opposite is City Hall Park, or the old town common. Recently renovated, the park boasts a wonderful ground etching chronicling New York City's history.

Continue up Broadway and turn right into Chambers St.

2 Chambers Street

This is the start of New York's 'Court Quarter'. On the right is the Tweed Courthouse, completed in 1878 at the then phenomenal cost of $12 million; its creator, politician William Marcy Tweed, was driven from office for corruption. Further along Chambers Street, on the left, is the ornate Surrogate's Court, also known as the Hall of Records.

Turn left into Centre St.

3 Centre Street

Across Centre Street is the Municipal Building, built in 1914 as the city government's first skyscraper. Happy-looking New Yorkers leaving the building have just obtained marriage licences. Centre Street veers right at Foley Square, where marble steps lead to the imposing entrance of the US Court House. Topped with a gilded pyramid, the building has witnessed many famous trials.

Across Centre Street is the hexagonal New York County Court House, in which the film *Twelve Angry Men* was shot.

Turn right on Leonard St, right into Baxter St, then cross Worth St to Cardinal Hayes Place and Pearl St. Follow Pearl under Brooklyn Bridge and turn left into Peck Slip. Follow the streets to the waterfront.

4 South Street Seaport

Featuring some of the oldest architecture in lower Manhattan, the South Street Seaport Historic District was created in 1967 from restored 19th-century waterfront buildings and piers (*see pp48–9*). Historic ships, including the square-rigged *Peking*, are docked at Pier 16. The Visitor Center is on the ground floor of Schermerhorn Row, a terrace of red-brick warehouses.

A ROOM WITH A VIEW

The best view of the Hudson is from the Winter Garden Atrium at the World Financial Center.

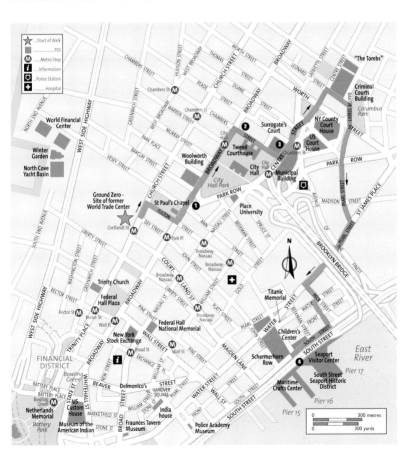

the 'flesh' of 0.3cm (⅛in)-thick hammered copper sheets which were bolted together.

The statue, paid for by the French, took 10 years to build. In 1884 it was dismantled, put into crates, loaded on to the French ship *Isre*, and eventually reassembled and mounted on its pedestal, paid for by the Americans, in 1886. It was dedicated by President Grover Cleveland on 28 October of that year, since when it has been passed by every ship entering New York Harbor. Millions of immigrants have been beckoned into the USA by the statue's 13m (42ft) right arm. Broken shackles lie at her feet, and her left hand holds a tablet inscribed with the date 4 July 1776 in French.

To visit the statue you need to buy a timed ticket at least 48 hours in

THE NEW COLOSSUS

Emma Lazarus' words, displayed at the site, encapsulate the spirit of Liberty: '...Here at our sea-washed sunset gates shall stand/A mighty woman with a torch, whose flame/Is the imprisoned lightning, and her name/ Mother of Exiles. From her beacon-hand/ Glows world-wide welcome; her mild eyes command/the air-bridged harbor that twin cities frame./"Keep ancient lands your storied pomp!" cries she/With silent lips. "Give me your tired, your poor,/Your huddled masses yearning to breathe free,/The wretched refuse of your teeming shore./Send these, the homeless, tempest-tost to me,/I lift my lamp beside the golden door!"'

advance (*see below*). Security is, not surprisingly, very strict these days and you won't be allowed to carry large bags around with you.

Once inside the statue, you will learn all about its history, have a chance to examine its incredible engineering, and be taken to the top where, after an elevator ride and a climb of the final 24 steps, you reach the observatory. Without a timed ticket you can still explore the island and take a ranger-led walking tour, see other exhibits and enjoy the shop and restaurant, but you won't be able to enter the statue itself.
Tel: (212) 363 7620; www.statueofliberty.org. Booking tickets for the Statue of Liberty: you can do this online at www.statuecruises.com or by phone on 1-877-523-9849 or (212) 269 5755, which is also the number for the current ferry schedules. Open: daily, 9am–5pm (longer in summer).

Trinity Church framed at one end of Wall Street

The stirring memorial wall for the dead of the Vietnam War

Closed: 25 Dec. Subway: 1, 9, N, R to South Ferry. Bus: M6, M15 to South Ferry, then Circle Line Statue of Liberty Ferry from the Battery on a regular schedule, 9.30am–5pm.
Subway: 4 & 5 to Bowling Green, N & R to Whitehall, or 1 to Rector St.

Trinity Church

The Anglican parish in Lower Manhattan was established in 1697 by charter from King William III. Public recitals and concerts are held on Thursdays at 1pm. The church has a free-entry museum. Tours are given. The present church is the third on the site. Opened in 1846, it was the tallest building in the city for the next half-century.
Broadway/Wall St. Museum tel: (212) 602 0800; www.trinitywallstreet.org. Open: Mon–Fri 7am–6pm, Sat

8am–4pm, Sun 7am–4pm.
Subway: Broadway/Wall St.

The Ukrainian Museum

Masses of hand-painted, vividly coloured *psanky* (Easter eggs), other folk art and ethnic jewellery, ceramics, costumes and textiles in a new, specially built facility.
222 E 6th St (2nd/3rd aves). Tel: (212) 228 0110; www.ukrainianmuseum.org. Open: Wed–Sun 11am–5pm. Admission charge. Subway: Astor Place.

Vietnam Veterans' Memorial

Excerpts from letters, diary entries and poems written by Americans who served in the Vietnam War are etched into this great memorial of granite and green glass blocks. There are also items from news despatches and public

(*Cont. on p60*)

Walk: TriBeCa

The name TriBeCa has been manufactured from the TRIangle BElow CAnal Street. A former sweatshop area of workshops and warehouses, TriBeCa today is an artistic neighbourhood with fashionable shops and restaurants.

Allow 1¼ hours.

Begin from Chambers St/Greenwich St (subway stations at Chambers St/Broadway and also Chambers St/Church St). Proceed up Greenwich St.

1 Greenwich Street

On the left is Washington Market Park, nearly 1.2ha (3 acres) of leisure facilities, on the site of a former food-market area. Further along, on the left, is the Independence Plaza, a residential and commercial complex. On the corner of Greenwich and Harrison streets is a row of 19th-century brick-built houses, moved to this site after being rescued from other parts of the area during demolition in the 1970s. At 375 Greenwich Street is the TriBeCa Film Center, a production company partly owned by actor Robert De Niro, who also has an interest in the street-level TriBeCa Grill, where well-known screen personalities are often seen.

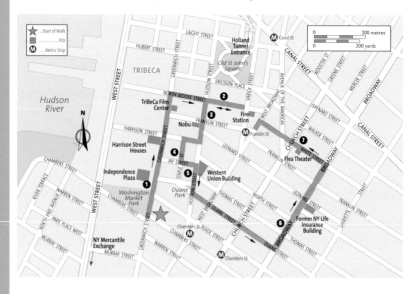

Continue northwards along Greenwich St. Turn right into North Moore St.

2 North Moore Street

The fire station at 14 North Moore Street featured prominently in the *Ghostbusters* films.
Double back along North Moore St and turn left into Hudson St.

3 Hudson Street

The entrance and exits of the Holland Tunnel are located just to the north. It is hard to believe now that this area was once a tranquil park dominated by the Church of St John. On the corner of Hudson and Franklin is the New York branch of the Nobu restaurant, a Manhattan favourite.
Turn right into Harrison St and left into Staple St.

4 Staple Street

This street is at the heart of the TriBeCa West Historic District. Commercial properties sprung up here in the nineteenth century.
Turn left into Jay St and return to Hudson St.

5 Hudson Street

Opposite the end of Jay Street is the Western Union Building, an Art Deco construction with a façade of bricks in 19 different colours. One block south is Duane Park, a small green area, all that remains of what was a Dutch family farm in the early to mid-1600s. It was acquired by New York City some 200 years ago for a few dollars.
Turn left into Duane St and walk east to Broadway. Turn left along Broadway.

6 Broadway

On the corner of Broadway and Leonard Street, the Victorian building which formerly housed the New York Life Insurance Company is topped by a tall clock tower which was added some 25 years after the offices were erected in 1870. As well as viewing the avant-garde art on display in the Clocktower Gallery, visitors may like to go up into the tower to see the clock's mechanism.
Continue up Broadway and turn left into White St.

7 White Street

At 41 White Street is the Flea Theater, a quirky and award-winning Off-Off-Broadway place. Founded in 1996, its stated aim was to create 'a joyful hell in a small space'.
Continue along White St, turn left along West Broadway to Franklin St subway station.

A zigzag of fire escapes in TriBeCa

statements relating to the war. The memorial is 20m (66ft) long and 4.9m (16ft) high.

Vietnam Veterans' Plaza, 55 Water St. Tel: (212) 693-1476;
www.nyvietnamveteransmemorial.org.
Subway: Wall St/William St.

Woolworth Building

Dubbed the 'Cathedral of Commerce', the 241m (792ft) white terracotta building was the world's tallest when it opened in 1913. It was the headquarters of the Woolworth corporation, whose founder, Frank Woolworth, made a fortune from the chain of 'nickel and dime' stores in which all merchandise was originally sold for either 5 or 10 cents. Many architecture students regard the building as the pinnacle of achievement in the genre. Its graceful lines are decorated with extravagant Gothic-style detail and its lobby is not to be missed. Sculpted reliefs in the four corners of the lobby include one of Woolworth counting out nickels and dimes with which to pay the architect Gilbert, who has a model of the building in his arms.

Broadway/Park Place. Subway: City Hall.

World Financial Center

New York's newest residential and commercial community, Battery Park City is dominated by the World Financial Center, and occupies a site alongside the Hudson River. The urban dream of a new city-within-a-city in Lower Manhattan, with office towers for international financial concerns and homes for 30,000 people, was formulated in the 1960s, designed by architects Cesar Pelli & Associates and opened in 1988. Today, it is all in place, within a short walk of Wall Street.

Battery Park City was drastically affected by the 11 September 2001 terrorist attacks on the neighbouring World Trade Center. Nonetheless, the area has bounced back as a resilient home for many, as the nearby Ground Zero site continues to be excavated. The surrounding area is in a state of flux, with visitors more welcome in some areas than others.

220 Vesey St. Tel: (212) 417 7000;
www.worldfinancialcenter.com

World Financial Center Building

Ground Zero

Until they were tragically destroyed on 11 September 2001 by two jet airliners in terrorist attacks, the World Trade Center (WTC) twin towers loomed over the Manhattan skyline as a symbol of the dynamic New York metropolis. More than 10ha (24 acres) of Battery Park City's 37ha (92 acres) were scooped out of the earth in order to create the Center.

Built by the Port Authority of New York and New Jersey as its international headquarters, WTC was best known for its 110-storey twin towers. On a clear day, the rooftop viewing point was the best place to view the city and had more than a quarter of a million visitors a year. Each tower was served by 23 high-speed lifts, able to reach the top in less than a minute. The towers played a starring role in the 1976 remake of *King Kong*.

For 50,000 people the towers were a workplace, housing at least 1,200 firms, representing more than 60 countries. At least 80,000 people visited on business every weekday.

The WTC was served by 22 restaurants and cafés, the most famous being the Windows on the World Restaurant at observation deck level. At concourse level was an indoor shopping mall.

The concept of a World Trade Center was born in the late 1950s, in a bid to resurrect what was a depressed area. The first tenants moved into one of the towers in 1970, and the WTC was dedicated in 1973. During the peak construction period there were 3,500 workers involved in the perilous job of erecting the towers.

On 4 July 2004, the cornerstone for One World Trade Center – formerly known as Freedom Tower – was laid. On the site of the previous World Trade Center, this new construction will be one of the world's tallest buildings when completed. It is due to be finished in 2013. In the meantime, there is a free public viewing wall at Ground Zero. Surrounding the site, this steel grid is flanked by large panels describing the events of 9/11.

The site will eventually be home to the National September 11 Memorial & Museum. The museum will give visitors the chance to see a collection of artifacts from the towers, photographs, personal effects from the victims and survivors, as well as recorded audio and video testimonials. The memorial will open before the tenth anniversary of the tragedy.

Yeshiva University Museum

Dramatic exhibits on Jewish history and art. Special events, live performances, films and holiday workshops.
Main galleries at Center for Jewish History: 15 W 16th St. Tel: (212) 294 8330; www.yumuseum.org. Open: Mon 3.30–8pm, Tue–Thur & Sun 11am–5pm, Wed 11am–8pm, Fri 11am–2.30pm. Admission charge. Guided tours by appointment.

MIDTOWN MANHATTAN
American Folk Museum

A 2,787sq m (30,000sq ft) exhibition space showcasing America's folk heritage – paintings, furniture, pottery and quilts.

45 W 53rd St (5th & 6th aves). Tel: (212) 265 1040; www.folkartmuseum.org. Open: Tue–Sun 10.30am–5.30pm, Fri 11am–7.30pm, closed Mon. Admission charge.

Carnegie Hall

This opera and concert venue was opened in 1891, when Tchaikovsky travelled from Russia for the first concert. Since then, many of the world's leading performers have packed the hall, among them Mahler, Caruso, Toscanini, Leonard Bernstein, Frank Sinatra and the Beatles. Some of the nation's greatest symphony orchestras have regular seasons here. The Isaac Stern Auditorium is the largest and

Jewish art and history are celebrated at the Yeshiva University Museum

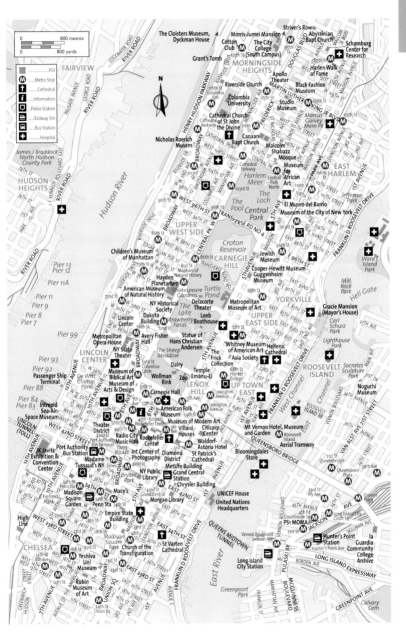

Carnegie Hall is at the centre of New York's musical life

best-known venue, seating over 2,800. The new Zankel flexible space holds around 600, and the Weill Recital Hall has a 268-person capacity.

154 W 57th St. Tel: (212) 247 7800; www.carnegiehall.org. Tours: Mon–Fri 11.30am, 12.30pm, 2pm & 3pm; Sat 11.30am & 12.30pm; Sun 12.30pm. Admission charge for guided tours. Tel: (212) 903 9765. Subway: 7th Ave/57th St.

Chrysler Building

An outstanding skyscraper in Art Deco architecture, it was briefly the world's tallest building until the Empire State Building went up in 1931. Its unusual stainless-steel-scaled spire, illuminated at night, makes it a familiar part of the New York skyline. Visitors are permitted into the lobby only, which has African marble walls. Ceiling murals depict workers constructing the spire. In the building is the Con Edison's Conservation Center, with hands-on exhibits, energy-saving and money-saving ideas, and experts at hand to answer questions on conservation.

At the corner of 405 Lexington Ave/42nd St. Tel: (212) 682 3070. Conservation Center open: mid-May–mid-Oct Mon–Fri, mid-Oct–mid-May Tue–Sat. Free admission. Subway: Grand Central Station.

Church of the Transfiguration

A John La Farge stained-glass window shows 19th-century actor Edwin Booth as Hamlet. Actors, writers and show-business people are among the worshippers here, and the church sponsors a small acting company. (Chinatown also has a Church of the Transfiguration in Mott Street. Opened in 1801 as a Lutheran Zion church, it is

The spire of the Chrysler Building is instantly identifiable in the New York skyline

The Empire State Building silhouetted against downtown Manhattan

now used by Chinese Roman Catholics.) *1 E 29th St. Tel: (212) 684 6770; www.littlechurch.org. Subway: Park Ave/28th St.*

Citicorp Center

Completed in 1979, this is an eye-catching building with a sharply sloping roof, intended for a solar energy project that was never completed. Among the world's tallest buildings, it has a three-level mall of shops and restaurants surrounding a skylit atrium known as The Market. Live music is played at weekends. At street level is St Peter's, a small modern church. *Lexington Ave/153 E 53rd St. Tel: (212) 559 2209. Open: daily. Subway: Lexington/3rd aves.*

Diamond District

A block at West 47th Street, between Fifth and Sixth avenues, comprises the wholesale jewellery trading district, dominated by bearded Orthodox Jews in black. Diamonds are cut and polished, jewellery repaired and set, and deals made above the ground-level shops. *Subway: 47th–50th sts/Rockefeller Center.*

Empire State Building

This 102-storey, 443m (1,454ft) Art Deco office-block structure – the height includes a TV transmitter mast – opened in 1931. Observatories at the 86th and 102nd levels give views of (*Cont. on p68*)

Manhattan architecture

Anyone with the eye to recognise it, can trace New York's modern history through its architecture – in some cases thanks to civic preservationists of the past. There were moves at one time, for example, to pull down most of seedy SoHo. The warehouses here and in neighbouring TriBeCa were saved by the noisy insistence of enough persuasive people to

Decorative panel in the Empire State lobby

influence the planners. The vast lofts of the sweatshops became fashionable homes and studios for artists, and industrial buildings became gracious residences.

One of New York's oldest surviving buildings is the Georgian-style St Paul's Chapel, dating from 1766. A few Federal-style buildings, including the Gracie Mansion, and a number of Greek Revival row houses remain from the 1820s and 1830s. Trinity Church, at the foot of Wall Street, is a good example of English Gothic.

New Yorkers are justifiably proud of their striking brownstone houses. Brownstone, quarried in Connecticut, first appeared in the 1840s as a façade on neo-Gothic and Italianate town houses, and was used in such profusion – thousands of brownstones were built in Manhattan and Brooklyn – that one critic dismissed it as 'chocolate sauce'.

It was, however, the introduction of 19th-century technology – cast-iron façades – that had the biggest impact on the city's architecture. Although lighter, its stronger method of construction enabled buildings to grow skywards, and to carry much classical ornamentation.

Seen from the air, the jumble of high-rises that comprise New York does not reveal the character of individual buildings

New York's first skyscraper was the triangular Flatiron Building, which went up in the early 1900s on Madison Square. By 1913, the 60-storey Woolworth Building on Broadway was hailed as the world's tallest. It was overshadowed by the 0.4km (¼-mile)-high twin towers of the 1973 World Trade Center, until the 11 September 2001 terrorist attacks brought them down. As sky-high buildings formed canyons in Midtown and Lower Manhattan, rules were imposed requiring buildings to be 'tiered' after a certain height to let the light in, lending them the flavour of the Art Deco style.

Woolworth Building

parts of four states, and the 86th floor has an outdoor promenade. Changing exhibitions are held in the lobby at the Fifth Avenue entrance. Children will enjoy the animated King Kong display and Eight Wonders of the World exhibit. Skyride is a thrilling simulated trip around the landmarks of Manhattan.

350 5th Ave/34th St. Tel: (212) 736 3100; www.esbnyc.com. Open: daily 8am–2am (last elevator up at 11.15pm).
Admission charge.
Subway: 6th Ave/34th St.

Grand Central Station

Not just a railway terminal, more an art form, and certainly a great engineering feat. Built in the Renaissance style over a ten-year period, it opened in 1913 with a vast main concourse – one of the world's largest rooms. It is 143m (470ft) long, and the barrel-vaulted ceiling, with 2,500 stars painted on a night sky background, is 46m (150ft) high. There are huge windows, and sculptures of Mercury, Athena and Hercules decorate the station clock. Elevated Park Avenue runs over the top of the Grand Central, which was declared a national landmark in 1978, thwarting a proposal to put up an office block at the site. Railway tracks at two levels carry more than 550 trains daily. The dining concourse at the tower level includes the popular Oyster Bar, and

Magnificent architecture of the Grand Central Station

offers a wide selection of cuisine. Free tours of the station are held at 12.30pm on Wednesdays.

42nd St/Lexington Ave.
Tel: (212) 532 4900;
(tours) (212) 935 3960
or (212) 883 2420;
www.grandcentralterminal.com.
Subway: Grand Central Station.

High Line

Formerly an elevated train track, the High Line is now a 2.3km (1.45-mile) pedestrian park that will eventually extend from Gansevoort Street to 30th Street. Right now, you can only explore up to 20th Street.

Located between Gansevoort Street in the Meatpacking District to 34th Street, between 10th and 11th aves.
Tel: (212) 500 6035;
www.thehighline.org.
Subway: L, A, C & E to 14th St;
C & E to 23rd St; 1, 2 or 3 to 14th St;
1 to 18th St or 23rd St.

International Center of Photography

Photography is very much the American art form. Here there are exhibitions of photographs from the 19th century to the present day, representing most of the world's leading practitioners, and also temporary shows of innovative work, some of it by local photographers.

1133 Ave of the Americas/43rd St.
Tel: (212) 857 0000; www.icp.org.
Open: Tue–Thur 10am–6pm, Fri
10am–8pm, Sat & Sun 10am–6pm.
Admission charge.

Intrepid Sea-Air-Space Museum

This famous World War II aircraft carrier is now a museum depicting events and armed conflicts around the world, up to and including the Gulf War, and the science and technology of the planes and ships involved. The world's fastest aircraft, spy-in-the-sky, and guided missile submarines are all represented here.

Pier 86, foot of W 46th St at Hudson River. Tel: (212) 245 0072;
www.intrepidmuseum.org.
Open: Apr–Sept Mon–Fri 10am–5pm,
Sat & Sun 10am–6pm. Oct–Mar Tue–Fri
10am–5pm, Sat & Sun 10am–5pm.
Closed Thanksgiving and Christmas.
Admission charge.
Subway: Fulton St/William St.

Madame Tussaud's New York

A $50 million attraction where you can spot nearly 200 celebrities.

324 W 42nd St (7th/8th aves).
Tel: (800) 246 8872; www.madame-tussauds.com. Open: Sun–Thur
10am–8pm, Fri & Sat 10am–10pm.
Admission charge.

Madison Square Garden

The world-famous sports and entertainment centre seats 20,000. It is also used as a convention centre and office complex, and is host to the New York Knicks (basketball) and New York Rangers (ice hockey).

In front of Madison Square Garden

4 Penn Plaza, near 33rd St.
Tel: (212) 307 7171 (TicketMaster);
www.thegarden.com. Subway: Penn
Station.

Morgan Library

This library houses the wonderful
collection of rare books and
manuscripts amassed by the wealthy
banker John Pierpont Morgan. Closed
in 2003 for refurbishment and
enlargement to a design by Renzo
Piano, it reopened in 2006 and now has
twice the exhibition space so that fewer
items need to be kept in storage.
Among the 10,000 and more items are
three Gutenberg Bibles, original
manuscripts by authors such as Mark
Twain and Charles Dickens, drawings
by Rembrandt, Rubens and Leonardo
da Vinci, and original musical scores by
Mozart and Beethoven.
225 Madison Ave/36th St.
Tel: (212) 685 0008;
www.morganlibrary.org.

Open: Tue–Thur 10.30am–5pm, Fri
10.30am–9pm, Sat 10am–6pm, Sun
11am–6pm. Admission charge. Subway:
33rd St.

Museum of Arts and Design

The nation's premier showcase for
contemporary craft presents exhibitions
of quilts, jewellery, rugs, architectural
ceramics, art-to-wear, handmade paper,
woodware and other crafts. Special
'Meet the Artist' programmes are
arranged. The permanent collection
demonstrates the emergence of the US
craft movement since World War II.
2 Columbus Cr/8th Ave. Tel: (212) 299
7777; www.madmuseum.org. Open: Tue,
Wed, Fri–Sun 10am–6pm, Thur
11am–9pm. Admission charge. Subway:
Columbus Cr/59th St.

Museum of Modern Art

Housed on six floors, the recently
renovated museum has one of the
world's foremost collections of art from

1880 to the present day. Outside there is a refreshing sculpture garden with trees and pools.
11 W 53rd St. Tel: (212) 708 9400; www.moma.org. Open: Sat–Mon, Wed & Thur 10.30am–5.30pm, Fri 10.30am–8pm. Admission charge. Subway: 5th Ave/53rd St.

New York Public Library

Free one-hour tours and changing exhibitions are held in this marble-fronted landmark Beaux Arts building where New Yorkers congregate on the steps on fine days to eat their packed lunches. The book collection is one of the world's five largest – more than 6 million volumes in the research section alone. The Reading Room is where Trotsky studied before the 1917 Russian Revolution.

The ornate Reading Room at the New York Public Library

5th Ave/42nd St. Tel: (212) 930 0800; www.nypl.org. Open: Mon & Thur–Sat 10am–6pm, Sun 1–5pm, Tues 10am–9pm. Subway: 42nd St/Grand Central Station.

Radio City Music Hall

This 1930s Art Deco landmark building, within the Rockefeller Center, claims a list of superlatives: world's biggest indoor theatre for rock concerts and revues; world's biggest chandelier over the staircase; world's largest contour curtain – it weighs about 3 tonnes – and a mighty Wurlitzer. It is also home to the Rockettes dance troupe. Backstage tours are conducted on most days.
1260 Ave of the Americas/50th St. Tel: (212) 307 7171; www.radiocity.com. Tours daily 11am–3pm. Admission charge. Subway: Rockefeller Center.

Rockefeller Center

Thinking big came naturally to financier John D Rockefeller Jr. In the late 1920s, in defiance of the thick cloud of depression hanging low over North America and the West, he decided to go ahead with a long-held ambition: to create an architectural business and entertainment complex in the centre of Manhattan.

The Rockefeller Center is a 19-building, 9ha (22-acre) complex providing a base for much of the nation's television programming, and headquarters for international corporations.

Rockefeller Center

On the entertainments side, the Radio City Music Hall (*see pp71 & 146*), with world-class performers on the stage, is based at the Center. Among a number of NBC-TV network programmes transmitted from studios in the complex is the early-morning Today show, tuned into by millions around the world.

John D Rockefeller (the D is for Davison), whose fortune came from the Standard Oil Company that he founded, was born in 1839, and was an old man when his plans for the Center were formulated.

One aspect of his dream, however, never became reality. He had dearly wanted to support a civic drive to provide a new home for the Metropolitan Opera within the Center. The harsh economic climate of the times, leading to the 1929 Wall Street Crash, forced him to put aside that project. However, even without it, the developers of the Rockefeller Center achieved what they set out to do – to construct a city-within-a-city, making optimum use of air, light and transportation facilities.

Upmarket shops selling a wide range of goods surround the Lower Plaza and are also at ground level of most of the Center's skyscrapers. Theatres and a variety of restaurants are dotted about.

Many visitors to New York City seek out the famed Rainbow Room for its panoramic views of the Manhattan skyline. Unfortunately, the restaurant

Underground concourses with shops and restaurants link the buildings. The Lower Plaza, where the flags of the United Nations fly, was created as a focal point. A promenade between the Plaza and Fifth Avenue is lined with beds of flowers, changing with the seasons, but always providing colour.

From October to April the Plaza features a skating rink. In the warm months it becomes a café-restaurant, presided over by a 5.5m (18ft) bronze figure of Prometheus, covered with gold leaf – one of the city's most photographed statues.

The flagship of the centre is the 70-storey Rockefeller Plaza skyscraper, and the boundaries of the complex extend from 47th Street to 51st Street, and between Fifth and Sixth avenues.

that was previously at the top of the GE Building is currently closed. Other eating options range from fine dining to fast food. Restaurants come and go, so check for the latest options online, by phone or at the information desk (*see below*). Current favourites include the Brasserie Ruhlmann at 45 Rockefeller Center (*www.brasserieruhlmann.com*), a classic Art Deco French brasserie owned by Jean Denoyer. If you're only interested in a snack or quick meal, there's everything from Ben & Jerry's to Yummy Sushi.

With the Rainbow Room closed, Rockefeller Center's observation decks are the next-best place to head for knock-out aerial views of the city. Known as Top of the Rock, these are on the 67th to the 70th floors and provide breathtaking panoramic views. The ones looking down on Central Park can't be seen from anywhere else in the city.

47th–52nd sts west of 5th Ave.
Tel: (212) 632 3975;
www.rockefellercenter.com.
Top of the Rock. Tel: (212) 698 2000;
www.topoftherocknyc.com. Open: daily
8am–midnight. Admission charge.
Information at 30 Rockefeller Plaza
(concourse level); call for opening hours.
Subway: Rockefeller Center.

The sumptuous statue of Prometheus dominates the Rockefeller Plaza

St Patrick's Cathedral

Seat of the Archdiocese of New York. The building of this Gothic-style structure, by James Renwick, began in 1858 and was completed in 1874.
5th Ave/50th St. Tel: (212) 753 2261; www.saintpatrickscathedral.org. Open: daily 6.30am–8.45pm. Subway: Rockefeller Center.

St Vartan Armenian Cathedral

Modelled on the lines of Armenian architecture of the 5th to 7th centuries, this building contains the Armenian Museum of Art and Antiquities, which has artefacts, art and manuscripts dating back to the 13th century. There is also a bookstore and gift shop.
2nd Ave at E 34th St. Tel: (212) 686 0710. Open: daily 10am–5pm. Sun service: 9.30am. Subway: Park Ave/33rd St.

Theater District

Historical landmarks still standing include the Martin Beck Theater, which

The façade of St Patrick's

staged premieres authored by such giants as Arthur Miller and Tennessee Williams; and the St James, where Lauren Bacall once worked as an usherette. Theater Row, a collection of Off-Broadway playhouses on 42nd Street, between Ninth and Tenth avenues, offers a good choice of productions and eating places.
Subway: Times Square.

UNICEF House

A permanent exhibition about children of all countries and what must be done to best preserve their rights.
3 UN Plaza/44th St. Tel: (212) 326 7000; www.unicef.org. Open: Mon–Fri 10am–4pm.

United Nations Headquarters

It took a group of architects six years to design the 168m (550ft)-high United Nations building on a 7ha (18-acre) site. Although geographically located in New York City, the UN headquarters lies in an international zone with its own post office. The guided tour takes an hour. It includes the Secretariat Building, the General Assembly Hall and Conference Wing.

If it all seems a little awe-inspiring, just remember that it is not only heads of state and top-name representatives of the nations of the world who gather here. It used to be possible to attend meetings of the General Assembly, but heightened security now means that to see the General Assembly you must take one

The streets around the UN commemorate champions of human rights

of the guided tours. These also take in the Security Council Chamber and the many works of art in the complex of buildings.

The Conference Building houses the Security Council Chamber, the Economic and Social Council and the Trusteeship Council. Visitors also see a

DINING AT THE UN

The UN building has a Delegates' Dining Room, where members of the public can book for lunch. Visitors could find themselves seated at a table next to the UN Secretary General. *Tel: (212) 963 7625; www.delegatesdiningroom.com*

post office where they can buy UN stamps for mail posted in the building. Many post letters to themselves for the sake of the stamp.

The decision to erect the UN building in New York was made after John D Rockefeller Jr donated $8.5 million towards the provision of a permanent site in the city for the headquarters. A team of architects from several nations, led by American Wallace Harrison, combined their talents to design the UN building between 1947 and 1953. It was completed in 1963.

(*Cont. on p78*)

Broadway and Off-Broadway

Once, there was only Broadway – that Great White Way of theatres clustered in the Times Square area. Here was the pre-war world of glamour and glitter, with big names in bright lights and more stars on stage than you could see in Manhattan's night sky. Then came Off-Broadway, a shadowy outer ring of lowlier playhouses, lesser players and cheaper tickets. Off-Off-

Catching a Broadway show is a must for many visitors to New York

Broadway was further out in every sense. But then the scene changed. Many of the old Broadway houses vanished in clouds of demolition dust, the Theater District extended west to Ninth Avenue and north to 53rd Street, and demarcation lines became blurred as standards rose and new talents emerged. The fact that a performance takes place in an Off-Broadway location does not necessarily mean that the audience will be sitting in dusty bargain seats, watching a show in which the prompt is busier than the players. The Off- or even Off-Off-Broadway show of today may be the smash hit of tomorrow. It may miss out Broadway altogether and go on to conquer the world. It has happened before. Indeed, these experimental theatre productions, staged in anything from a one-bulb garage to a converted church, are the very best in the world.

In recent years Broadway has also embraced the music of artists who are better known for their chart-topping records and live concert tours than for their show-tune pedigrees. The music of pop icons Paul Simon and Billy Joel could have been foreseen as a natural fit for Broadway. But who would

Broadway gave the musical to the world – and the Great White Way remains synonymous with all the gloss and the glamour of high-quality showmanship

guess that Bob Dylan and even Green Day would have their moment on Broadway? Paul Simon's *The Capeman* wasn't a smash success during its run in 1998, but the songs from the show have endured as fan favourites. In 2002 Twyla Tharp's dance musical *Movin' Out*, based on the music of Billy Joel, debuted and ran for years. 2006 saw a tribute to Dylan with *The Times They Are A-Changing*. And, most recently in 2010, rock band Green Day's album 'American Idiot' was adapted for the Broadway audience. In this way, Broadway has endured and developed shows that would appeal to new fans as well as stalwarts.

Nostalgia nevertheless rules along the Great White Way, and echoes of the past can still be heard in the wings, orchestra pits and dressing rooms of the few theatres still surviving from those heady pre-TV days. The St James, at 246 W 44th Street, saw Lauren Bacall begin her Broadway career in the 1940s – as an usherette. Barbra Streisand took her first bow at the Shubert Theater, 225 W 44th Street, where *A Chorus Line* ran for a record-breaking 15 years. Among historic productions staged, since 1924, at the Martin Beck Theatre, 302 W 45th Street, was the premiere of Eugene O'Neill's *The Iceman Cometh*.

There are restaurants, shops selling goods from many parts of the world, and a crafts shop. Also worth seeing are works of art donated by member countries, such as the *Reclining Figure*, a bronze statue from the Henry Moore Foundation, the *Statue of Peace* from the former Yugoslavia, and the 'knotted gun' sculpture that depicts a gun with its muzzle tied up to denote peace, which was created by Swedish artist Carl Fredrik Reuterswärd. Beautiful rose gardens overlook the East River.

The organisation developed from the pre-war League of Nations which had failed to prevent World War II and was disbanded in 1946. During the war Britain, the USA, the Soviet Union, France and China got together with a view to forming a new world organisation.

On New Year's Day 1942, the representatives of 26 countries signed the Declaration of the United Nations in Washington, DC, but it was not until April 1945 that the UN was officially founded, at the Conference on International Organisation in San Francisco, when representatives of 50 nations unanimously adopted the UN Charter.

In that same month, US President Franklin D Roosevelt died. His widow, Eleanor, was to chair the UN Commission on Human Rights from 1947 to 1951.

The Waldorf-Astoria: if you wait long enough, you might spot someone famous here

The first Secretary General of the United Nations was Trygve Lie, a Norwegian politician, elected on 1 February 1946. He held the office until 1952. Today, a total of 192 states have UN membership.

Four purposes are listed in the UN Charter: to maintain international peace and security; to encourage friendly relations between states, based on the principle of equal rights and self-determination for all; to promote international cooperation in solving social, economic and cultural problems; and to serve as an agency through which member states can act to achieve these goals.

Business is conducted in six official languages – Arabic, Chinese, English, French, Russian and Spanish.
1st Ave/45th–46th sts. Tel: (tours) (212) 963 8687; www.un.org. Open: Mon–Fri 9.45am–4.45pm. Admission charge for guided tours. Subway: Grand Central Station.

Villard Houses

A must for architecture aficionados, these three brownstone mansions date from 1886, and were built in palazzo style for newspaper publisher Henry Villard. The buildings form an early Renaissance-style courtyard with elaborate wrought iron, and are now integrated with the New York Palace Hotel. The interiors are in pristine condition.
455 Madison Ave/50th St. Subway: Lexington Ave/51st St.

Waldorf-Astoria Hotel

As much a part of New York as the Empire State Building or the Statue of Liberty, the 1,245-room Waldorf-Astoria is an Art Deco masterpiece in its own right. This was where the Waldorf salad was invented. The hotel still draws the rich and famous – as well as honeymoon couples from Middle America – and its luxurious lobby continues to be a major meeting point.
301 Park Ave/50th St.
Tel: (212) 355 3000;
www.waldorfnewyork.com.
Subway: Grand Central Station.

Whitney Museum Altria

Small picture gallery, with changing exhibitions on modern themes, and a sculpture court. (*See also the Whitney Museum of American Art p97.*)
120 Park Ave/42nd St. Tel: (917) 663 2453. Open: Mon–Fri 11am–6pm, Thur 11am–7.30pm. Sculpture court open: Mon–Sat 7.30am–9.30pm, Sun 11am–7pm. Free admission.
Subway: Grand Central Station/42nd St.

UPPER MANHATTAN
American Museum of Natural History/Hayden Planetarium

Permanent exhibitions in different halls are devoted to the peoples of Asia, South America, the Pacific and Africa, Mexico, Central America and to Native Americans. There is the famous collection of dinosaur skeletons, as well as sections on minerals and meteorites, gems, molluscs, African and Asian animals and birds. The museum houses a collection of some 36 million artefacts – surely something for everyone. There is a calendar of special events, and an IMAX Theater with a 4-storey screen.

The Planetarium has the Space Show, computerised special effects and live shows for children on some weekends.

Central Park West/E 79th St.
Tel: (212) 769 5100; www.amnh.org.
Open: daily 10am–5.45pm. Closed:
Thanksgiving & Christmas Day.
Museum: Admission charge suggested to
visitors. The museum is part of the
City Pass programme.
IMAX: Central Park West/81st St.
Tel: (212) 769 5200. Open: see
American Museum of Natural History
for times. Admission charge compulsory.
SuperSaver Admission Packages include
the IMAX. Subway: 81st St/Central
Park West.

Asia Society

The Society's dynamic programme of activities shares a modern interior with John D Rockefeller's Asian art collection.

725 Park Ave/70th St.
Tel: (212) 288 6400; www.asiasociety.org.
Open: Tue–Sun 11am–6pm.
Subway: E 68th St.

Cathedral Church of St John the Divine

Begun in 1892 and still under construction, the church seems

The magnificent window in St John the Divine

destined to be the world's largest neo-Gothic cathedral. The nave alone will be twice as big as a full-size American football pitch, seating 5,000 people. The Episcopal cathedral stands in 5.3ha (13 acres), and has a shelter for the homeless, a gymnasium, biblical garden, museum of religious art and a gift shop. Art exhibitions and free concerts are also held in addition to regular services and special events. Specially trained stone cutters, drawn from the local community, can be seen at work as the cathedral is supported in traditional style by stonemasonry, rather than today's steel framework. There is a poets' corner modelled after Westminster Abbey's, honouring American writers.

1047 Amsterdam Ave/112th St.
Tel: (212) 316 7540;
www.stjohndivine.org.
Open: Mon–Sat 7am–6pm, Sun
7am–7pm. Tours: Tue–Sat 11am &
1pm, Sun 2pm. Subway: 110th St/
Cathedral Parkway.

Central Park

A placid green rectangle set among the crazed order of city streets, Central Park covers a surprisingly large area – 341ha (843 acres) of land that must cause nightmares for property developers working out its worth in terms of the rent they could charge for each square metre. In the 1850s, however, there were doubts about the city's wisdom in purchasing a precinct of rocks, swamp and shantytown at what was then the exorbitant price of $7,500 an acre.

The idea of creating a central reserve of grass, trees and tranquillity for the rapidly growing city was first mooted in 1844 by poet and journalist William Cullen Bryant, but it took many years to persuade the authorities not to give in to the demands of developers.

Finally, a competition was staged to find the best plan for the park, and the winners – landscape designer Frederick Law Olmsted and architect Calvert Vaux – started the construction work in 1860.

It took Olmsted and Vaux 16 years to accomplish their dream of creating a bucolic Valhalla in the middle of what was already one of the world's greatest cities, to say nothing of $14 million and the shifting around of some 424,750m^3 (5 million cubic yards) of earth and rock.

Their achievement in transforming an area of near-wilderness into rolling countryside, with thick woodlands, lakes and lawns – even farm buildings and a meadow on which sheep really did graze – was widely acclaimed, and they were

Manhattan

An oasis ringed by sentinel skyscrapers

commissioned to create landscapes in other parts of the USA, including Capitol Hill in Washington, DC.

The stroke of genius in the scheme drawn up by Olmsted and Vaux was the creation of transverse roads which passed underneath a meandering network of footpaths, enabling through-traffic to cross the park without disturbing the peace of visitors.

Central Park's layout today is much the same as its designers intended. Acts of civic vandalism, which turned areas of greenery into hard-surfaced playgrounds and fenced-off games pitches, have been mitigated to some extent since 1980, by extensive restoration.

Despite its reputation as a haunt of muggers and junkies, the park has the city's lowest crime rate – policing has been increased dramatically in recent years – and its popularity is obvious, especially during summer weekends when people turn out in their hundreds. Even in the depths of winter, it takes no more than a light fall of overnight snow to bring out the sledges and skis.

Summer or winter, the southern quarter of the park is the place for family fun. Here, within a few minutes' walk of Columbus Circle or Grand Army Plaza, you can have the kites and frisbees flying, get your skates on, sunbathe or visit the zoo animals.

Information about the park can be obtained from the Dairy Visitor Center or online at *www.centralpark.com*, while just north of here, the Sheep Meadow is a popular place for picnics and free concerts on summer evenings. Further north still, bikes and boats can be rented at the Loeb Boathouse

Central Park resplendent in its autumnal glory

(*www.thecentralparkboathouse.com*), and Shakespeare is performed at the Delacorte Theater. Nearby, the Shakespeare Garden is filled with plants mentioned by the Bard.

Another favourite picnic area for the crowds is the Great Lawn, parallel with the Metropolitan Museum of Art. Above this is the Reservoir, more often than not ringed with joggers.

Less popular, and therefore quieter, is the northern quarter, with its pools and three formal gardens donated by the wealthy Vanderbilt family.

Central Park Zoo and Wildlife Conservation Center

Wildlife from polar, temperate and tropical zones is housed in uncaged habitats. More than 400 animals and birds from around 130 species are represented here. Nearby is a children's petting zoo.

E 64th St/5th Ave. Tel: (212) 861 6030; www.centralparkzoo.com. Open: Apr–Oct weekdays 10am–5pm, weekends & holidays 10am–5.30pm; Nov–Mar daily 10am–4.30pm. Admission charge. Subway: 68th St/Hunter College Station.

Children's Museum of Manhattan

The multimedia show in the 'Brainatorium' demonstrates how the brain works. Nature, art and science are all presented entertainingly. There is a hands-on media centre and TV studio, as well as programmes for pre-school children. Dancing, music, theatre and storytelling sessions and workshops are held at weekends and during holidays.

Tisch Building, 212 W 83rd St. Tel: (212) 721 1234; www.cmom.org. Open: Tue–Sun & on school holidays 10am–5pm. Admission charge; extra for performances and workshops. Subway: 81st St/Central Park West.

The Cloisters Museum

This branch of the Metropolitan Museum of Art overlooking the Hudson River specialises in medieval art and architecture. Colonnaded walks lead between French and Spanish cloisters, a 12th-century chapterhouse, a chapel and other imported monastic buildings.

Fort Tryon Park. Tel: (212) 923 3700; www.metmuseum.org. Open: Mar–Oct Tue–Sun 9.30am–5.15pm; Nov–Feb Tue–Sun 9.30am–4.45pm. Admission charge. Subway: 190th St.

Cooper-Hewitt Museum

Incorporating the Smithsonian Institution's National Museum of Design, this is the only museum in the USA devoted to contemporary and historical design. The collection covers textiles, jewellery and other ornamental works, and architectural drawings.

2 E 91st St/5th Ave. Tel: (212) 849 8400; www.cooperhewitt.org. Open: Mon–Fri 10am–5pm, Sat 10am–6pm, Sun 11am–6pm. Admission charge. Subway: Lexington Ave/86th St.

West Side story

The West End of the early 19th century comprised small distinct villages, and remained largely undeveloped. It was the coming of the subway that enhanced its appeal and urbanised it through the proliferation of apartment blocks. In the 1890s, Columbia University relocated here. Artists and academics shared the neighbourhood with the equally lively mob, which played and fought its flashy way through the early decades of the 20th century. Development and construction ceased from the early 1930s through to the early 1980s and the Upper West Side's popularity waned, making it an undesirable address.

A fearsome reputation spread swiftly when the film version of Leonard Bernstein's musical *West Side Story* (based on the Romeo and Juliet story) burst on to the wide screens of the world in 1961. The menacing glint of knives, defiant young toughs strutting the decaying streets and spoiling for a fight – these images of poverty, degradation and violence were conveyed with gritty realism. But the film was also an epitaph for the area it portrayed. The streets in which many of the scenes were actually shot were already condemned, and when the camera crews moved out the bulldozers moved in. The mouldering tenements and sweatshops, the rubble-strewn battlefields that were once playgrounds, the dying shops and schools, were all razed to make way for the splendour of the

Zabar's Cheese Department

Far removed from its 1960s reputation for violence, the West Side today is marked by its multi-ethnic society and institutions such as Zabar's (left) and the Lincoln Center (above)

Lincoln Center, the main aim of which was to raise the tone of the area.

Today's West Side story is one of culture and multi-ethnic coexistence. There are still some slums, but in the main the area bordered by Central Park on the east, the Hudson River on the west, and by 59th and 114th streets to the south and north is comfortable and safe, with trendy boutiques and restaurants and smart apartment blocks.

It seems that the Upper West Side is now settling into the intended lifestyle of a place that has attracted as residents the likes of Thomas Wolfe, Enrico Caruso, Igor Stravinsky, Arturo Toscanini, John Lennon, Yoko Ono and many other luminaries.

Walk: Central Park

Central Park is much larger than it seems – almost 341ha (843 acres) of lawns, lakes and woodlands, where visitors can follow pursuits as diverse as skating and birdwatching, jogging and croquet, cycling or simply sitting still.

Allow 2 hours.

Begin at W 72nd St subway station, cross Central Park West and West Drive, and follow the path to Strawberry Fields.

1 Strawberry Fields

This hillside garden is dedicated to John Lennon, murdered in December 1980 outside the Dakota Building just across Central Park West. Lennon's wife, Yoko Ono, still lives at the Dakota, and the Strawberry Fields site is maintained through an endowment she has made.

Head north, following either of the paths skirting West Drive (the lakeside one is best), then turn right on to the path on the north side of the 79th St Transverse.

2 Cottage and Castle

The wooden chalet is the Swedish Cottage, one of the park's many

The John Lennon Memorial

architectural oddities. Another is the nearby Belvedere Castle, a whimsical amalgam of medieval styles built in 1872 to enhance the view from across the Lake. The castle itself affords a view of the Delacorte Theater and the park's Great Lawn beyond.

Between cottage and castle is the Shakespeare Garden, with plants mentioned in the Bard's works.

Continue east, crossing the intersection of 79th St Transverse and East Drive. Take the path south to Conservatory Water.

3 Conservatory Water

Remote-control model boats compete in exciting races on Saturday mornings in summer; it is a pleasant spot at any time. Children can climb all over Lewis Carroll's Alice and the other Wonderland characters in the bronze sculpture at the northern end of the pond, or listen to tales being told at the foot of a statue of Hans Christian Andersen on the west side.

Head west along the path that crosses East Drive and leads to the Loeb Boathouse.

Cleopatra's Needle and the Metropolitan Museum of Art are some other sights on this walk.

4 The Lake

Rowing boats and gondolas (and bikes) can be rented at the Loeb Boathouse, which also has a reasonable restaurant. Exercise apart, the lake provides an excellent foreground for photographs, paintings or sketches of New York's various profiles. A good place is the cast-iron Bow Bridge, which crosses the narrow neck of water between the smaller and larger sections of the Lake. Midway between boathouse and bridge, the Bethesda Fountain, set on a strikingly paved terrace, provides further photographic opportunities.

From the fountain take the tiled tunnel south to pass under the 72nd St Transverse and reach The Mall.

5 The Mall

At the northern end of The Mall is the Bandshell, where summer concerts and other performances take place. The Mall itself, some 274m (300yds) long, is known as the 'Literary Walk' because it is also lined with the statues of world-famous writers. West of The Mall is the Sheep Meadow, 6ha (15 acres) of open space in which anything noisier or more energetic than picnicking is banned.

At the foot of The Mall, cross to the western side of East Drive.

6 Southeast Corner

Just below the 65th Street Transverse is the Dairy, now used as the park's visitor center. South of the Dairy is the Wollman Memorial Rink, where New Yorkers skate. The often photographed Pond is in this corner of the park.

Follow the path to the Pond's southern edge and turn left to complete the walk at Grand Army Plaza.

Home to the Frick Collection

Dyckman House

Furnished in original 18th-century style, this is the only remaining Dutch farmhouse in Manhattan. It was presented to the city by the Dyckman family in 1915.
4881 Broadway/204th St.
Tel: (212) 304 9422;
www.dyckmanfarmhouse.org.
Open: Wed–Sat 11am–4pm, Sun noon–4pm. Subway: 190th St.
Admission charge.

El Museo del Barrio

The only museum in the United States exclusively devoted to the art and culture of Puerto Rico and Latin America. Founded in 1969 and based in Harlem, the museum provides a fascinating insight into the neighbourhood and its people.
1230 5th Ave/104th St. Tel: (212) 831 7272; www.elmuseo.org. Open: Tue–Sun 11am–6pm. Donation suggested. Subway: Lexington Ave/103rd St.

Frick Collection

More like a home than most major galleries, this 1935 Beaux Arts mansion is much as it was when industrialist Henry C Frick lived here, with a fortune in European Old Masters from the 14th to 19th centuries. When your feet are tired, relax among the fountains and greenery in the glass-ceilinged courtyard.
1 E 70th St. Tel: (212) 288 0700;
www.frick.org. Open: Tue–Sat 10am–6pm, Sun 11am–5pm. Admission charge. Subway: Lexington Ave/68th St.

Gracie Mansion (1799)

Federal-style frame house in Carl Schurz Park that has been the official residence of New York's mayors since 1942 (*see p98*). Period items loaned from private collections are displayed, and there is a permanent 'Merchants to Mayors' exhibition in the basement.
East End Ave at 89th St.
Tel: (212) 639 9675; www.nyc.gov.
Open: end Mar–mid-Nov. Tours on Wed by appointment only. Children and students free.
Subway: Lexington Ave/86th St.

Grant's Tomb

Near Columbia University, this is the granite mausoleum where Civil War general Ulysses S Grant, twice US president, and his wife are buried. The tomb is a national monument, with photographs and memorabilia.
Riverside Drive/122nd St.
Tel: (212) 666 1640. Open: daily

9am–5pm. Closed: Thanksgiving, Christmas and New Year's Day. Subway: Broadway/125th St.

Guggenheim Museum

Modern art sometimes raises eyebrows, and when the museum opened in 1959 Frank Lloyd Wright's setting for it certainly did. The museum displays some of the priceless works which 19th-century multimillionaire Solomon Guggenheim collected from Europe, as well as some rare photographs of his contemporaries. Themed and other temporary exhibitions of the work of 20th-century artists are held from time to time.
1071 5th Ave/E 89th St.
Tel: (212) 423 3500;

www.guggenheim.org.
Open: Sun–Wed 10am–5.45pm, Fri 10am–5.45pm & Sat 10am–7.45pm. Admission charge. Subway: Lexington Ave/86th St.

Harlem

The scene of civil rights riots during the 1960s, and still associated in many minds with urban dereliction, Harlem is undergoing restoration. It remains a mecca for black culture. You can reach it by bus or the subway, though at night it would be wiser to take a taxi. Bus and walking tours are available (*see p183*). Some Harlem streets have been co-named out of respect for the area's black heritage, such as Lenox Avenue, which now shares its name

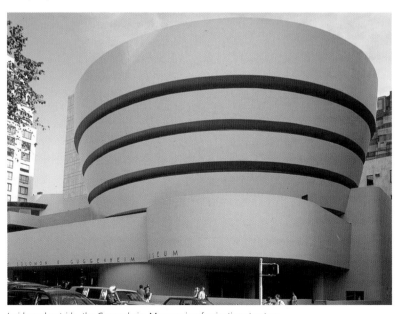

Inside and outside, the Guggenheim Museum is a fascinating structure

Harlem brownstones

with Malcolm X Boulevard. The area
is famous for its nightlife – check
publications like *New York Magazine*
for what's happening.

Abyssinian Baptist Church

Built in Gothic style, this bluestone
building is noted less for its
architecture than for its former
incumbent, the Revd Adam Clayton
Powell Jr, America's first black
congressman, and for its lively Sunday
services with a belt-it-out choir and
fire-and-brimstone sermons.
*132 Odell Clark Pl (W 137th/138th sts).
Tel: (212) 862 7474;
www.abyssinian.org.
Sunday services: 9am & 11am.*

Apollo Theater

Opened in 1913 as a music hall for
whites only, the Apollo's stage was
ultimately graced by such artistes as
Ella Fitzgerald, Billie Holiday, Aretha
Franklin, Count Basie and Duke
Ellington. It has lively amateur
performances on Wednesday nights.
*253 W 125th St. Tel: (212) 531 5305;
www.apollotheater.org*

Canaan Baptist Church of Christ

Gospel music at its best, performed
during Sunday services.
*132 W 116th St. Tel: (212) 866 0301;
www.cbccnyc.org. Sunday services:
8am & 11am. Subway: W 116th St
(Malcolm X Blvd, or 8th Ave).*

The Cotton Club

Although the Cotton Club is now at
656 West 125th Street, its original
location can still be seen at the
junction of 142nd Street and Lenox
Avenue. This is where, in 1923, boxer
Jack Johnson sold his Club DeLux to
gangster Owney Madden, who
renamed it The Cotton Club. Stars
like Duke Ellington, Bing Crosby and
Lena Horne all played or drank there,
and its fame extended into fiction
and film.
*656 West 125th St. Tel: (212) 663 7980;
www.cottonclub-newyork.com*

The Harlem Walk of Fame

Plaques on the pavement honour
some of the area's famous residents
from past and present, including

leading sports, music, literary and political figures.
W 135th St (5th/St Nicholas aves).

Malcolm Shabazz Mosque

Topped by an aluminium dome, this former casino has been a place of worship for Muslims in Harlem since the 1960s. Malcolm X used to preach here.
102 W 116th St.
Subway: 116th St/Malcolm X Blvd.

Marcus Garvey Park

A rocky area cutting across Fifth Avenue between 120th and 124th streets, the park honours the Jamaican black leader who headed a back-to-Africa movement between the two World Wars. It is surrounded by many splendid late 19th-century houses in the Mount Morris Historic District.
Subway: W or E 116th St.

Schomburg Center for Research in Black Culture

More than 100,000 books, photographs and documents collected by Arthur Schomburg, a Puerto Rican immigrant, are on display.
515 Malcolm X Blvd. Tel: (212) 491 2200;
www.nypl.org/locations/schomburg.
Open: Mon–Thur noon–8pm, Thur & Fri 11am–6pm, but departments vary so phone to check. Free admission. Subway: 135th St/Malcolm X Blvd.

Strivers' Row

These two rows were built in the 1890s to show that attractive dwellings could be built cheaply, and since the end of World War I they have been occupied by black middle-class professionals who, from the start, were seen by their less fortunate neighbours as strivers after the good life.
W 138th & W 139th sts (7th/8th aves).

Studio Museum

A small art museum housing a large collection of paintings, sculptures and photographs. The museum also has changing exhibitions and a programme of lectures. There is also a gift shop.
144 W 125th St. Tel: (212) 864 4500;
www.studiomuseum.org.
Open: Wed–Fri & Sun noon–6pm, Sat 10am–6pm. Suggested donation.

Jewish Museum

This is the USA's most significant institution devoted to Jewish history and culture. The museum holds the largest collection of Jewish ceremonial objects in the western hemisphere, many of which were rescued from European synagogues before World War II. Also displayed here are historical exhibits, artworks and manuscripts. Exhibits demonstrate the poverty of Lower East Side immigrants and the Holocaust sufferings.
1109 5th Ave/92nd St. Tel: (212) 423 3200; www.thejewishmuseum.org.
Open: Sun–Tue 11am–5.45pm, Thur 11am–8pm, Sat 11am–5.45pm.
Admission charge, Sat free. Subway: Lexington Ave/96th St.

African Caribbean connection

It began with Christopher Columbus, who brought the first black people to America in 1492. Over the next four centuries millions of black Africans were transported to the New World as slaves. By the early 1700s, New York had become the trading centre for slaves to be sent on to Latin America and the Caribbean region to work on sugar, coffee and cotton plantations. Though slavery was not initially a major part of New York's economy, it had become big business by the 1730s. African New Yorkers worked as house servants, cleared forests, built roads and helped on farms. During British rule, a considerable number became skilled artisans, blacksmiths, coopers and carpenters, working on contract for their owners. Later, European immigration scattered the African American population to isolated pockets in the city.

The colourful costumes make the Labor Day carnival well worth a look

The black community is an integral part of city life

The movement of black people into the city, which had started with runaway slaves from the South even before the Civil War, accelerated during the 1920s, and continued even faster after World War II when Puerto Ricans also started to arrive. Caribbean immigration became prevalent in the 1960s.

Today many of these cultures celebrate their heritage during annual festivals and parades. Popular events include the Puerto Rican Day Parade in June and the spectacular West Indian American Day Parade, part of the Carnival on Brooklyn's Eastern Parkway, which takes place each Labor Day weekend in September.

Basketball stars in the making in Central Park

Lincoln Center for the Performing Arts

Six separate concert halls and theatres seating a total of 18,000, built in the 1960s, cover eight blocks. The centre is home to the New York Philharmonic, the Metropolitan Opera Company and the New York City Opera and Ballet.

Broadway/64th St. Tel: (212) 875 5350; www.lincolncenter.org. Admission charge for daily tours 10.30am–4.30pm. Subway: Broadway/Lincoln Center.

Metropolitan Opera House and Backstage Tour

A 90-minute tour of scenery and costume shops, stage areas and rehearsal facilities gives a captivating insight into the working of the Opera House. Reservations required, call weekdays.

Lincoln Center. Tel: (212) 582 3512; (tours) (212) 769 7020; www.operaed.org. Tours: Oct–Jun, by reservation. Admission charge. Subway: Broadway/Lincoln Center.

Special exhibitions at the Met are a regular feature of the New York cultural scene

Metropolitan Museum of Art

To do justice to the Metropolitan Museum of Art, time is needed. Since only a limited amount of culture can be absorbed in, say, three or four hours, what you really need is to devote several half-days to the Met until you have sated your particular appetite, at least until you are next in New York. The Met is a vast treasure house, occupying four blocks, and containing more than three million priceless exhibits.

Self-discipline is required to get the best out of each visit. Study a plan of the three floors before you launch yourself out of the magnificent Great Hall and decide which of your interests you want to indulge on each occasion. For instance, if 20th-century art is your forte, you will note that it is exhibited in the same position on each floor.

The museum is closed on Mondays. From Tuesday to Friday, free tours of the highlights of the museum leave the Great Hall about every 25 minutes, less often at weekends.

Inevitably, as happens with such a huge collection, not all sections are permanently open, so anyone planning a visit with one vital interest in mind would be advised to enquire in advance whether it is currently on display.

Because of the time it takes to deposit and retrieve outerwear, most people carry their overcoats around with them in winter, or even wear them in the well-heated galleries. If it is practical, dress lightly and, of course, wear your most comfortable shoes.

The Met is one of several museums that has a suggested contribution instead of a fixed admission charge. That contribution also allows admission on the same day to The Cloisters, reconstructed from European medieval buildings, up north in Tryon Park, overlooking the Hudson River. It contains the Met's medieval collection (*see p83*). In summer, an hourly shuttle bus runs between the two.

The museum houses works of art from ancient civilisations to the present day. Among them are hundreds of world-famous masterpieces. As well as galleries of painting and sculpture, the museum has displays of tapestries, musical instruments, costumes and ornaments.

The five major collections are European Painting, American Painting, Primitive Art, Medieval Painting and Egyptian Antiquities. A hall on the ground floor re-creates the Temple of Dendera (15 BC), built by the Roman emperor Augustus. The Primitive Art collection is in one of four new wings: the Michael C Rockefeller Wing, a memorial to Nelson Rockefeller's son, who disappeared in New Guinea in 1961. Splendidly ornamental armour, heraldic banners and the finest collections of Japanese arms and armour outside Japan are exhibited in the Arms and Armor galleries.

The American Wing includes rooms dedicated to various periods in the nation's history. One of them is by Frank Lloyd Wright, designer of that controversial modern building the Guggenheim Museum.

The Twentieth Century Art collection has some riveting works from Europe and America in the Lila Acheson Wallis Wing. Above it, on the roof, open in the summer, is a garden of contemporary sculpture.

The design of the museum includes courtyard gardens with soaring glass roofs and delightfully restful green areas with interesting statuary. Tiffany glass can be seen along the balcony by the American Wing garden.

Also welcome are the unexpected glimpses of Central Park from various angles, that appear like living canvases of landscapes and people.

The final pleasure is seeking a memento or an art book from the museum shops.
1000 5th Ave/82nd St.
Tel: (212) 535 7710;
www.metmuseum.org. Open: Tue–Thur & Sun 9.30am–5.30pm, Fri & Sat 9.30am–9pm. Closed: Mon, Thanksgiving, Christmas Day, New Year's Day. Donation suggested. Subway: 86th St/Lexington Ave.

Morris-Jumel Mansion

Built in 1765 by Colonel and Mrs Roger Morris as a country home, this mansion was used briefly in 1776 as George Washington's headquarters. Non-historians may find more of interest in the love life of a later resident, Mrs Eliza Jumel.
65 Jumel Terrace, 160th St/St Nicholas Ave. Tel: (212) 923 8008;
www.morrisjumel.org.
Open: Wed–Sun 10am–4pm.
Admission charge.
Subway: St Nicholas Ave/163rd St.

Mount Vernon Hotel Museum and Garden

A 1799 carriage house, converted into a country hotel in 1826, is now a museum of 19th-century New York City history and decorative arts. There are guided tours of period rooms.
421 E 61st St. Tel: (212) 838 6878;
www.mvhm.org. Open: Tue–Sun 11am–4pm. Closed: holidays. Admission charge. Subway: 59th St.

Museum for African Art

This exciting collection is mounting exhibitions at various venues around the city until they move into their new permanent home in 2011.
1280 5th Ave/110th St.
www.africanart.org

Museum of Biblical Art

Rare historic Bibles, unusual current editions in English and other languages, and the Dead Sea Scrolls are among the exhibits.
1865 Broadway/61st St, near Lincoln Center. Tel: (212) 408 1500;
www.mobia.org. Open: Wed, Fri–Sun noon–6pm, Thur noon–8pm. Donation suggested. Subway: 59th St.

Museum of the City of New York

Presents the city's development from a Dutch trading post to today's bustling metropolis. Exhibitions of furniture, artworks, toys, dolls' houses and costumes.

1220 5th Ave/103rd St.
Tel: (212) 534 1672; www.mcny.org.
Open: Tue–Sun 10am–5pm.
Donation suggested.
Subway: Lexington Ave/103rd St.

New York Historical Society

American art and antiques, advertising art, original Audubon watercolours of birds and other wildlife, Tiffany lamps and antique toys. Also, more than 4 million manuscripts, prints and rare books.

170 Central Park West/77th St.
Tel: (212) 873 3400; www.nyhistory.org.
Open: Tue–Fri noon–8pm, Sat 10am–6pm, Sun 11am–5.45pm.
Admission charge. Subway: 79th St.

Riverside Church

A 1930s inter-denominational church with a carillon of 74 bells – the world's largest – in its 109m (356ft) tower. A small charge is made to take the elevator 20 storeys up to see the view. A socially and politically aware church, Riverside opens its doors to a range of community events and music, dance and drama.

490 Riverside Drive at 120th/122nd sts.
Tel: (212) 870 6700;
www.theriversidechurchny.org. Free tours
of church after Sunday service; tours start

12.15pm approx, but times vary.
Subway: Broadway/116th St.

Temple Emanu-El

Another New York 'world's largest'. This is the Reform Jewish synagogue in the Upper East Side. It seats 2,500 worshippers. It was built in 1929 and influenced by several architectural styles.

1 E 65th St. Tel: (212) 744 1400;
www.emanuelnyc.org.
Open: Sun–Thur 10am–4.30pm.
Free admission. Subway: Lexington Ave/E 68th St.

Whitney Museum of American Art

There is always something exciting to see here, especially in alternate years (those with odd numbers) in the spring, when the exhibitions pinpoint what new things are happening on the American art scene. The Whitney, founded in 1930 by Gertrude Vanderbilt Whitney, concentrates on the 20th century. Its galleries display a variety of styles and themes from a wide range of artists. There are changing exhibitions, and film and video programmes are presented.

945 Madison Ave/75th St.
Tel: (212) 570 3600; www.whitney.org.
Open: Wed–Thur & Sat–Sun 11am–6pm, Fri 1–9pm. Closed: Mon, Tue, Independence Day, Christmas Day & New Year's Day.
Admission charge (Fri 6–9pm pay what you wish). Subway: Lexington Ave/ 77th St.

Walk: Yorkville

Yorkville, Upper East Side, retains much of its Central European character – immigrants from Germany, Austria, Hungary and the former Czechoslovakia have been settled here since the 1870s. There are beer halls, delicatessens, and restaurants serving Wiener schnitzel and red cabbage.

Allow 1½ hours.

Begin at E 86th St subway station. Walk briskly or catch a bus the 0.8km (½ mile) to the eastern end of E 86th St.

1 Henderson Place Historic District

Located between York Avenue and East End Avenue, Henderson Place has a row of 24 small, turreted Queen Anne-style cottages of brick and timber, built as servants' quarters in 1882, and now among the city's most desirable residences. The servants' employers lived in nearby mansions, which have long since vanished.
Cross East End Ave to Carl Schurz Park.

2 Carl Schurz Park

Overlooking the East River, the park affords a view of the Triborough Bridge and Hell's Gate, where treacherous currents of the Harlem River, Long Island Sound and New York Harbor merge. On the opposite side of the river is the borough of Queens. The park honours a versatile German immigrant who served as a US diplomat, a Union Army major general and a senator representing Missouri. Appointed Secretary of the Interior in President John Quincy Adams's government, he also later became editor of *Harper's Weekly*. He died in 1906.
Walk north through the park to Gracie Mansion.

3 Gracie Mansion

Built in the late 18th century, Gracie Mansion (*see p88*) was the home of wealthy merchant Archibald Gracie. The City of New York acquired it in 1887, using it as a museum. Since the 1930s when the popular Fiorello LaGuardia resided here, it has been the official residence of the Mayor of New York.
Leave Carl Schurz Park at E 88th St and head west.

4 East 88th Street

Between First and Second avenues is the French Gothic-style Church of the Holy Trinity – flying buttresses, arches, gargoyles and stained-glass windows in the style of the Middle Ages. Organ recitals and concerts of classical music are presented in the church. Between Park and Fifth avenues, 88th Street marks the southern border of the Carnegie Hill area, one of the city's most exclusive residential neighbourhoods. The area is named after millionaire Andrew Carnegie, who set a trend – followed by the Astors and Vanderbilts – by building a mansion in what were the unfashionable northern outskirts of Manhattan in 1901.

Continue west on E 88th St, then turn right into 5th Ave.

5 Fifth Avenue

This part of Fifth Avenue is known as Museum Mile. It stretches from the Frick Collection at 70th Street to El Museo del Barrio at 105th Street. Frank Lloyd Wright's controversial spiral building, the Guggenheim Museum between 88th and 89th streets, presents an unusual, exciting and practical way of looking at art. The museum's six floors (pedants will say there is just one, wound like a watchspring) display works by Chagall, Klee and Picasso.

Next, on 89th/90th, comes the National Academy of Design, an elegant mansion housing a collection of American art. At 91st Street is the Smithsonian Institution's National Design Museum, better known as the Cooper-Hewitt Museum. This is the 64-room mansion built by Andrew Carnegie. A block north is the Jewish Museum with four galleries on Jewish heritage (*see p91*).

Turn right on to E 96th St and end the walk at the 96th St subway.

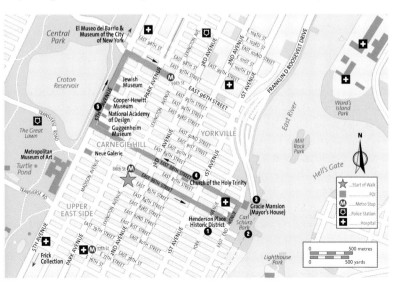

The Bronx

A Danish immigrant, Johannes Bronck, founded the Bronx when he bought 202ha (500 acres) of land from the Dutch West India Company in 1639. The only borough connected to the mainland, the Bronx was originally inhabited by the wealthy, but through the decades gradually acquired a rather rundown reputation. Its population is about 1.4 million, now comprising several ethnic groups who settled here. A large community of Italians lives in the Belmont area.

Unless you are in the crowd at the Yankee Stadium and the right team wins, or at the Zoo where the animals live in something like their natural habitat, you do not go to the Bronx specifically to be cheered and uplifted. Indeed, one of the local attractions is a cemetery, and another is the cottage where Edgar Allan Poe spent a sad time towards the end of his life.

On the other hand, if you disregard the warnings of New Yorkers, you can explore much of the Bronx in complete safety and feel rewarded for the effort. The Zoo and Wave Hill – a former estate – and the New York Botanical Garden are green havens. Where else will you ever come across a snuff mill?

To get to these delights, take the subway and travel right through the South Bronx – the trains come out into the daylight here. More northerly parts have gained favour in recent years as a place to set up home.

The one part of the South Bronx that draws New Yorkers by the thousand is the **Yankee Stadium**, the first subway station reached from Manhattan. The Yankees baseball team moved from Harlem to the Bronx in 1923. Team stalwart Babe Ruth played for the Yankees for 15 years, and his statue, along with those of other greats like Joe DiMaggio, can be seen at the stadium.

Arthur Avenue Retail Market
A marketplace with several dozen stalls. Fruit and vegetables are piled high and big cheeses and strings of spicy sausages dangle temptingly before the eyes.
2344 Arthur Ave. Subway: Fordham Rd.

Bartow-Pell Mansion
Built between 1836 and 1842, the mansion is preserved as a historical museum and national landmark. There are several hiking trails in the park.
Pelham Bay Park. 895 Shore Rd.
Tel: (718) 885 1461;
www.bartowpellmansionmuseum.org.
Open: Wed, Sat & Sun noon–4pm.
Admission charge.

Bronx Heritage Trail

Guided tours of three historical houses. *Bronx County Historical Society, 3309 Bainbridge Ave. Tel: (718) 881 8900; www.bronxhistoricalsociety.org. Open: Mon–Fri 9am–5pm, Sat 10am–4pm, Sun 1–5pm, weekdays by appointment.*

Bronx Museum of the Arts

Permanent art exhibits ranging from Old Masters to new local talent, as well as changing exhibitions. *1040 Grand Concourse/165th St. Tel: (718) 681 6000; www.bronxmuseum.org. Open: Thur, Sat & Sun 11am–6pm, Fri 11am–8pm. Donation suggested. Subway: 161st St/Grand Concourse.*

Bronx Supreme Court House

This was one of the locations for the film *The Bonfire of the Vanities*. *Subway: Grand Concourse.*

New York Zoological Gardens (Bronx Zoo)

The largest urban zoo in the USA, with nearly 4,000 creatures covering nearly 700 species on 107ha (265 acres). The animals enjoy simulated indoor and outdoor habitats, like Jungle World, the Congo Gorilla Forest and Tiger Mountain. There are also Himalayan Highlands (with snow leopard and panda), African Plains, Wolf Woods, a World of Darkness (with nocturnal

Experience something of the African Plains in the Bronx Zoo

animals), a World of Birds, a mouse house and a huge wilderness area devoted to the elephants of Wild Asia, which can be seen from the Bengali Express monorail and the Safari cable car from May to October.
Bronx River Parkway/Fordham Rd. Tel: (718) 367 1010; www.bronxzoo.com. Open: Mon–Fri 10am–5pm, Sat & Sun 10am–5.30pm. Admission charge Thur–Tue; donation suggested on Wed. Subway: East Tremont Ave.

City Island

Set in Long Island Sound, off the borough's eastern shore, this is a fishing, boatbuilding and yachting community, with an assortment of seafood restaurants. There are gingerbread houses, bungalows with stained-glass windows and an historical nautical museum at 190 Fordham Road. A narrow causeway connects the island with Pelham Bay Park. Several yachts entered for the America's Cup, including the *Intrepid*, a winner in the 1960s, are moored here.
Nautical Museum, 190 Fordham Rd. Tel: (718) 885 0008; www.cityislandmuseum.org. Open: Sat & Sun 1–5pm. Free admission.

Enrico Fermi Cultural Center

Housed within the Belmont branch of New York City Library. Books on the achievements and contributions of Italian immigrants to local life can be found in the Heritage Collection here.

610 E 186th St. Tel: (718) 933 6410; www.nypl.org. Subway: Fordham Rd.

Fordham University

Formerly a self-contained village, now skirting the Grand Concourse, Fordham has been settled over the past 150 years by Irish, Germans, Italians, Jews, African Caribbeans, Hispanics and, more recently, refugees from Cambodia and Albania. Today, Fordham University, on a 34ha (85-acre) site near the Botanical Garden, is one of several campuses in the Bronx and has 7,500 students. The university dates back to 1841, the dominant building being a massive pile, Keating Hall.
Subway: Fordham Rd.

Hall of Fame for Great Americans

Noted Americans of the past from many walks of life are commemorated in this granite colonnade designed by Stanford White. The landmark structure houses busts of presidents, statesmen, scientists, artists and humanitarians.
Tours can be booked in advance. Bronx Community College, W 181st St/University Ave. Tel: (718) 289 5161; www.bcc.cuny.edu/halloffame. Open: daily 10am–5pm. Free admission. Subway: Bedford Park Blvd/Lehman College.

Lehman Center for the Performing Arts

A major entertainment centre for music, dance and theatre.

250 Bedford Park Blvd.
Tel: (718) 960 8833;
www.lehmancenter.org. Subway: Bedford
Park Blvd/Lehman College.

Museum of Bronx History
See Valentine-Varian House, p104.

New York Botanical Garden
Inspired by Kew Gardens during a visit
to England in 1889, botanists Dr
Nathaniel Lord and his wife Elizabeth
Britton returned to New York
determined to create something similar.
In only two years, with a deep gorge of
the Bronx River and 16ha (40 acres) of

original woodland providing special
features, the basics were completed.
Today, 11 splendid galleries form the
Enid A Haupt Conservatory, with
orchids, ferns, palms, cacti and flowers
of the tropics. Another building on the
101ha (250-acre) site is the 1840
Lorillard Snuff Mill, where tobacco was
ground for snuff, with the petals of
roses growing nearby contributing to
the blend. The museum building
houses a herbarium, with many
thousands of dried plants. There is also
a library and a garden shop where
visitors can obtain a guide to the
gardens. The Erph Compass Garden,

The Botanical Garden provides a welcome sense of rural tranquillity

with cobblestones marking the points of the compass, is just one of the brilliant collections of flowers.
Southern Blvd south of Mosholu Parkway in Bronx Park, adjacent to Bronx Zoo. Tel: (718) 817 8700; www.nybg.org. Open: Nov–Mar Tue–Sun 10am–5pm; Apr–Oct daily 10am–6pm. Admission charge. Subway: Bedford Park Blvd/ Grand Concourse.

Pelham Bay Park

More than 809ha (2,000 acres) of land form Pelham Bay Park, part of a tract bought from the Native Americans by Thomas Pell in 1654. There is 1.6km (1 mile) of beach, a riding school and boat basin, and facilities for cycling, picnicking, fishing and tennis.

Poe Cottage

Edgar Allan Poe moved here from Manhattan with his sick wife, Virginia, in the hope that her health would improve, but she succumbed to tuberculosis. Her deathbed and his rocking chair are in the sparsely furnished cottage where Poe lived for three years. After moving out from here, Poe soon died in mysterious

NEW YORK IN BLOOM

Special flower displays are held at various times of the year at the New York Botanical Garden in the Bronx. First is a spring bulb show in February, followed by a daffodil and magnolia weekend in early April. April also brings the New York Orchid Show. A bonsai exhibition is held in October.

circumstances. Administered together with the Valentine-Varian House (*see below*) by the Bronx County Historical Society.
East Kingsbridge Rd/Grand Concourse. Tel: (718) 881 8900; www.bronxhistoricalsociety.org. Open: Sat 10am–4pm, Sun 1–5pm. Closed: Mon–Fri. Admission charge. Subway: Kingsbridge Rd.

Riverdale

In contrast to South Bronx, this is a region above University Heights overlooking the Hudson River and the New Jersey Palisades, where wealthy 19th-century Manhattanites built spacious summer homes.

Valentine-Varian House

Fieldstone farmhouse built by blacksmith Isaac Valentine in 1758. It houses the Museum of Bronx History.
3266 Bainbridge Ave/E 208th St. Tel: (718) 881 8900; www. bronxhistoricalsociety.org. Open: for weekday tours by appointment, Sat 10am–4pm, Sun 1–5pm. Admission charge.

Van Cortlandt Park

Caribbean immigrants play cricket in this extensive park in the northwest of the Bronx, part of a 1646 Dutch land grant. Golf, tennis, riding, boating and other recreational facilities are available.

Wave Hill

A Riverdale area estate of 11ha (28 acres) bought in 1903 by George W

Perkins. It has been home at different times to Mark Twain, Theodore Roosevelt and Arturo Toscanini. A manor house dates from 1844. Perkins built another, and created gardens with greenhouses, rare plants and a sculpture garden. Concerts are performed here.

W 249th/Independence Ave. Tel: (718) 549 3200; www.wavehill.org.
Open: mid-Apr to mid-Oct Tue–Sun 9am–5.30pm; mid-Oct to mid-Apr Tue–Sun 9am–4.30pm. Free admission Sat Dec–Feb; rest of the year, Tue all day, Sat before noon.

Woodlawn Cemetery

Spot the famous names in this 130-year-old cemetery with some over-the-top edifices – a Who's Where guide can be obtained at the cemetery office. Duke Ellington is here, and so is F W Woolworth in an Egyptian-style palace.

233rd St/Webster Ave. Tel: (718) 920 0500; www.thewoodlawncemetery.org. Open: daily 8.30am–5pm. Free admission. Subway: Woodlawn.

Yankee Stadium

Home of the New York Yankees baseball team, the new Yankee Stadium opened in 2009 across the street from the original facility that was built in 1923 by Jacob Ruppert, owner of the Yankees at that time. Tours are available.

161st St/River Ave. Tel: (718) 293 6000; www.yankees.mlb.com. Office open: Mon–Sat 9am–5pm, Sun 10am–5pm. Subway: Yankee Stadium.

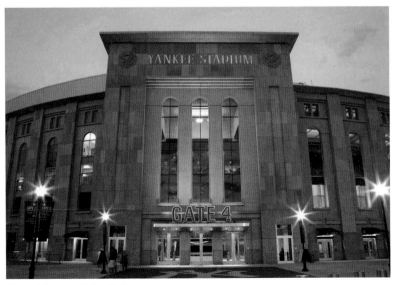

The sparkling new Yankee Stadium

The European influx

The variety of eating and other commercial establishments testifies to the rich mix of cultures found in New York: Le Figaro in Greenwich Village

The Native Americans were cunning enough to sell to the first Dutch settlers an island, Manhattan, which didn't belong to them. The Dutch gave way to the British and New Amsterdam became New York. After the Revolution, independent America opened its doors and New York's ethnic diversification accelerated. In the mid-19th century came the mass waves of European migration into New York, caused by the social upheaval of the Napoleonic wars, the potato famines in Ireland and Germany, and the unsettling effects of the Industrial Revolution. Initially, the Irish and German immigrants predominated, but by the early 1900s, Jews and Italians comprised the largest groups.

The descendants of New York's original immigrants – the Dutch, English and Germans – are hard to find nowadays, although Yorkville still has a strong German flavour. The Irish, too, are scattered, but there are enclaves still in parts of Queens and the Bronx.

Close-knit Jewish communities are to be found in the Bronx, Brooklyn and Queens, with sizeable groupings of the strictly Orthodox Hasidic Jews in Williamsburg, Crown Heights and Borough Park in Brooklyn. Of the once-teeming Jewish community on Manhattan's Lower East Side, only a few traces remain. Many Italian-Americans, too, have moved to the suburbs, but the city still has a number of recognisable neighbourhoods. Although once threatened by encroachment from adjoining Chinatown, Little Italy manages to maintain its identity and continues to thrive.

Today the city blends cultures while retaining certain traditions of each immigrant faction. There is a large population of proud Puerto Ricans, many individuals from southeast Asian countries, and a mixture of residents hailing from sub-Saharan Africa.

Little Italy

Brooklyn

With 2½ million inhabitants – a million more than Manhattan – Brooklyn is the largest of the five boroughs in terms of population. Many visitors get no further than elegant Brooklyn Heights, unless they take a trip to Coney Island or Brighton Beach, but the borough's attractions are well worth exploring.

Borough Hall

Brooklyn's seat of government is a sober Greek Revival building, part of the Brooklyn Heights civic centre. Tours are led by an architectural historian.
209 Joralemon St. Tel: (718) 875 4047. Open: Tue 1pm for tours only. Free admission. Subway: Borough Hall.

Brighton Beach

Situated at the eastern end of Coney Island, the resort is known as 'Little Odessa' because it is home to some 30,000 Russian émigrés, the largest such community in the USA, many of whom arrived during the 1970s. Noisy vodka drinking abounds and there are lots of inexpensive restaurants with Georgian menus.
Subway: Brighton Beach.

Brooklyn Academy of Music

Founded in 1859, BAM, as aficionados call it, is an outstanding cultural centre, with four theatres.
30 Lafayette Ave. Tel: (718) 636 4100; www.bam.org. Subway: Atlantic Ave/Pacific St.

Brooklyn Botanic Garden

Covering 21ha (52 acres) and noted for its Japanese, fragrance and herb gardens.
1000 Washington Ave. Tel: (718) 623 7200; www.bbg.org. Open: Tue–Fri 8am–6pm, Sat & Sun 10am–6pm. Admission charge. Subway: Botanic Gardens.

Brooklyn Bridge

Opened in 1883, the bridge was one of the finest Victorian engineering achievements, and still ranks among the world's greatest suspension spans. Superb views from its upper walkway.
Subway: High St/Brooklyn Bridge.

Brooklyn Children's Museum

Lots of hands-on experiences and more than 40,000 authentic ethnological, natural history and other artefacts.

145 Brooklyn Ave. Tel: (718) 735 4400; www.brooklynkids.org. Open: Sept–Jun Wed–Sun 11am–6pm, Jul & Aug Tue–Sun 11am–6pm. Admission charge. Subway: Kingston/Throop aves.

Brooklyn Heights Historic District

A 50-block area reflecting the architectural styles of 19th-century America. (*See Walk pp110–11.*)
Walk across Brooklyn Bridge from Lower Manhattan, or ride the subway to Brooklyn Bridge/High St or Clark St.

Brooklyn History Museum

Located in the Brooklyn Heights Historic District, the museum features Brooklyn Dodgers' baseball exhibits, and displays on Coney Island, Brooklyn Bridge and Brooklyn Navy Yard.
*128 Pierrepont St, Brooklyn Heights, at the corner of Clinton St & Pierrepont St. Tel: (718) 222 4111; www.brooklynhistory.org. Open: Sun & Wed–Fri noon–5pm, Sat 10am–5pm. Admission charge.
Subway: Clark St.*

Brooklyn Museum of Art

One of the nation's leading museums and the second largest in NY. The Egyptian collection is said to be even finer than those in Cairo and the British Museum in London.
200 Eastern Parkway. Tel: (718) 638 5000; www.brooklynmuseum.org. Open: Wed–Fri 10am–5pm, Sat & Sun 11am–6pm (1st Sat of month 11am–11pm). Donation suggested.

Subway: Eastern Parkway/Brooklyn Museum.

Cobble Hill

A sedate neighbourhood of brownstone houses and red-brick terraces. Jenny Jerome, mother of British prime minister Sir Winston Churchill, was born at 197 Amity Street.
Subway: Borough Hall.

Coney Island

At one time, Coney Island was the most famous amusement resort in the world. It has more than 5km (3 miles) of beach. Among the amusements are the Wonder Wheel, the Cyclone roller coaster and the New York Aquarium.
Subway: Coney Island.

The Esplanade

Better known as 'The Promenade', this narrow strip of parkway overlooks the East River. Visitors contemplate the view of Manhattan as the joggers pound by.
Located at the East River end of Pierrepont St. Subway: Clark St.

Brooklyn Heights Historic District

Walk: Brooklyn Heights

Gracious living of the past is still evident from the brownstone houses and opulent avenues of Brooklyn Heights, a 50-block historic district.

Allow 2 hours.

Begin at the Manhattan end of Brooklyn Bridge. Walk across the bridge's wooden promenade. Leave by the left fork, go under the bridge to Cadman Plaza West, following it westwards to Old Fulton St.

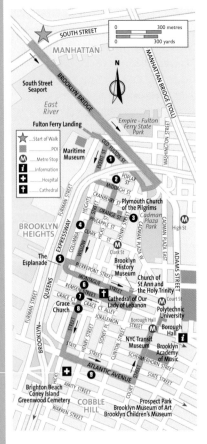

1 Old Fulton Street

Although in a rather drab area, Old Fulton Street leads to the part-cobbled Fulton Ferry Landing (*see p114*), from which there is a good view of Manhattan's skyline. It is opposite South Street Seaport, and is named after the steam ferry that Robert Fulton operated to transport Brooklyn's businessmen between home and Wall Street before the bridge.

Return along Old Fulton St, turning right at Everit St into Columbia Heights, then left into Middagh St.

2 Middagh Street

Number 24 Middagh Street, at the corner of Willow Street, is the oldest home in the area, a timber-built, 'gingerbread' house dating from the 1820s. (Gingerbread refers to the decorative wooden embellishment to the buildings' exteriors.) Middagh Street was named after a prominent 19th-century family, one of whom so disliked this practice that she named several local streets after trees and fruit instead.

Continue along Middagh, turning right at Hicks St and left at Orange St.

3 Orange Street

Plymouth Church of the Pilgrims is where the clergyman Henry Ward Beecher preached passionately for the abolition of slavery, and harboured runaways from the South before the Civil War.

Return across Hicks St, turning left into Willow St.

4 Willow Street

Henry Ward Beecher lived at No 22, a classic-style brownstone. There is also a row of 17th-century Federal houses believed to have been part of the 'underground railroad', a clandestine organisation that helped fugitive slaves.

Turn right on to Pierrepont St and cross Columbia Heights to the Brooklyn Heights Esplanade.

5 The Esplanade

Also known as 'The Promenade' (*see p109*), this leads through a narrow park providing the best view of Lower Manhattan.

Continue south along The Esplanade, turning left into Montague St.

6 Montague Street

This is a vibrant shopping street with a wide choice of national cuisines. Some famous writers have lived in the area,

including Arthur Miller, Truman Capote, W H Auden and Thomas Wolfe. Recently restored, the first stained-glass windows made in the USA can be seen at the Church of St Anne and the Holy Trinity at the corner of Montague and Clinton streets.

Turn right into Clinton St and right again into Remsen St.

7 Remsen Street

At No 113 Remsen Street is the Maronite Cathedral of Our Lady of Lebanon, built in Romanesque revival style and containing fitments from the SS *Normandie*, wrecked in 1943.

Turn left into Hicks St.

8 Hicks Street

Halfway between Remsen and Joralemon streets is Grace Court Alley, which contains a couple of dozen dignified mews homes. Further on Hicks Street is Grace Church, designed in Gothic Revival style in the mid-1990s by the architect Richard Upjohn.

Continue south along Hicks St, cross State St and turn left into Atlantic Ave.

9 Atlantic Avenue

Lebanese, Syrian and Yemeni eateries and stores form a Middle Eastern quarter located between Hicks and Court streets.

Turn left into Court St. Continue to Joralemon St, where the return journey to Manhattan can be made from Borough Hall subway station.

Brooklyn lifestyle

There was a time when residents of Manhattan, if they thought about it at all, regarded Brooklyn as no more than an urban dormitory on the opposite shore of the East River. Not any more. Brooklyn has come to be recognised for what it has, in fact, always been: a lively community with an identity uniquely its own, some handsome and highly desirable residential areas, and a vibrant mix of ethnic and cultural heritages.

Until 1898, when, after the opening of the Brooklyn Bridge spanning the East River, it was annexed into Metropolitan New York, Brooklyn was a city in its own right, covering 199sq km (77sq miles), and composed of six main towns and a number of small villages. If it were still independent, it would be the third-largest city in the USA. It has a population a million more than that of Manhattan.

Homes from a more gracious age in tree-lined Brooklyn Heights

Its neighbourhoods have managed to retain their individuality. Brooklyn Heights, the historic district with its very pretty streets, has a clear identity – a little snooty, perhaps, here and there – but you have only to move a few blocks to find something totally different. At Cobble Hill, for instance, bits of the Yemen, Syria and Lebanon have been dumped along a stretch of Atlantic Avenue – a Middle East bazaar of restaurants serving kebabs, hummus, couscous and the like, and shops rich with the scent of spices, roasting coffee and baking bread. These days Williamsburg – near Greenpoint, Bedford-Stuyvesant and Bushwick – is the main draw in Brooklyn. Young couples and families are moving to the area that is

Soaring elegance in Brooklyn Heights

known for its vibrant art, music and culinary scenes.

A traditional New York deli

Fulton Ferry Landing

Commuter ferries from Manhattan docked here before Brooklyn Bridge was built. There are plans to restore the area, turning surrounding warehouses into a museum and shopping mall. Great views of the bridge and Lower Manhattan, especially from eateries in Restaurant Row.

At the foot of Old Fulton St, reached by way of Cadman Plaza West.
Subway: High St/Brooklyn Bridge.

Grand Army Plaza

A dramatic circular open space at the entrance of Prospect Park (*see opposite page*), from which radiate Eastern Parkway, Prospect Park West, and Vanderbilt and Flatbush avenues. The Soldiers' and Sailors' Memorial Arch is modelled on the Arc de Triomphe in Paris, and honours the Union forces who were victors in the Civil War. The arch is topped by a dramatic sculpture of a chariot drawn by four horses, and inside are reliefs of presidents Abraham Lincoln and Ulysses S Grant.

Subway: Grand Army Plaza.

Greenwood Cemetery

More entertaining than you might imagine, this huge cemetery contains many elaborate tombs, and makes an interesting place to walk.

500 W 25th St/5th Ave.
Tel: (718) 768 7300; www.green-wood.com. Subway: 25th St.

Harbor Defense Museum

A collection of coastal armaments, uniforms and equipment going back to the 18th century.

Fort Hamilton, at the Brooklyn end of Verrazano-Narrows Bridge.
Tel: (718) 630 4349; www.harbordefensemuseum.com.
Open: Mon–Fri 10am–4pm, Sat 10am–2pm. Free admission.
Subway: 95th St/Fort Hamilton.

Lefferts Homestead

A Dutch Colonial farmhouse, built in 1776 and now housing a museum, the homestead is inside Prospect Park (*see opposite page*). It features period furniture and there is a programme of temporary exhibitions.

Flatbush Ave/Empire Blvd, Prospect Park.
Tel: (718) 965 6505. Open: Thur–Sun noon–5pm; in winter Sat & Sun and school holidays noon–4pm. Free admission. Subway: Prospect Park.

New York Aquarium for Wildlife Conservation

A large collection of rare and colourful fish, whales, seals and penguins. Dolphins, sea lions and electric eels perform for the public's entertainment.

602 Surf Ave/W 8th St, Coney Island.
Tel: (718) 265 3474;
www.nyaquarium.com.
Open: Apr–May, Sept & Oct Mon–Fri 10am–5pm, Sat, Sun & holidays 10am–5.30pm; Jun–Aug Mon–Fri 10am–6pm, Sat, Sun & holidays

10am–7pm; Nov–Mar daily
10am–4.30pm. Admission charge.
Subway: New York Aquarium.

New York Transit Museum
Set in a disused 1930s subway station
that was recently refurbished, the
museum features 80 years of transit
memorabilia from the great age of
public transportation.
*Boerum Place/Schermerhorn St,
Brooklyn Heights. Tel: (718) 694 1600;
http://mta.info/mta/museum/index.html.
Open: Tue–Fri 10am–4pm, Sat & Sun
noon–5pm. Admission charge. Subway:
Borough Hall.*

Plymouth Church of the Pilgrims
A large, simple church built in the 19th
century, this was where the preacher
Henry Ward Beecher led his campaign
against slavery before the Civil War.
The church was a mainline station on
the 'underground railroad' that
smuggled slaves to freedom. A great
campaigning orator, Beecher brought
many influential and famous
worshippers to the church, including
Mark Twain and Abraham Lincoln.

*75 Hicks St at Orange St. Tel: (718) 624
4743; www.plymouthchurch.org. Tours
are available following the Sun 11am
service or by appointment.
Subway: Clark St.*

Prospect Park
Landscaped by the same team that
designed Central Park, Olmsted and
Vaux, the park covers 213ha (526 acres)
within which can be found a zoo, music
grove, boating lakes and a skating rink.
The Friends of Prospect Park is a group
of nature lovers committed to caring
for the trees in the park.
*Its main entrance is from Grand Army
Plaza. Tel: (718) 965 8951;
www.prospectpark.org. Open: daily
5am–1am. Subway: Grand Army Plaza.*

Sheepshead Bay
An inlet marking the end of Brooklyn
and the start of Coney Island, the bay is
a busy deep-sea fishing centre, with
boats available for charter on piers
along Emmons Avenue. The avenue is a
lively place by day or night, with
waterside bars and restaurants.
Subway: Sheepshead Bay.

A breath of sea air at Sheepshead Bay

Long Island

Commuter traffic jams aside, no part of Long Island is much more than two hours by car from Manhattan, yet the island's 193km (120-mile) length is rich in diversity: sandy beaches, rich farmland and historic towns..

African American Museum

Exhibits display the history, cultural heritage and contributions of African-American Long Islanders, including special displays from the Smithsonian Institution and Brooklyn Museum.
110 N Franklin St, Hempstead, south of Garden City. Tel: (516) 572 0730; www.aamoflongisland.org. Open: Tue–Sat 10am–5pm. Free admission.

Cold Spring Harbor Whaling Museum

Nineteenth-century whaling exhibits, including 400 pieces of scrimshaw (whalebone carvings).
279 Main St, North Shore. Tel: (516) 367 3418; www.cshwhalingmuseum.org. Open: Tue–Sun 11am–5pm, Jun–Aug also on Mon. Closed: holidays. Admission charge.

Cradle of Aviation

Air and space museum with vintage aircraft and space exploration vehicles.
Mitchel Field, Garden City.
Tel: (516) 572 4111; www.cradleofaviation.org. Open: daily 9.30am–5pm. Admission charge.

Garvies Point Museum and Preserve

Archaeology and geology exhibits of coastal New York State. Nature trails.
50 Barry Dr, Glen Cove, Western North Shore. Tel: (516) 571 8010; www.garviespointmuseum.com. Open: Tue–Sat 10am–4pm. Closed: Sun, Mon, and holidays. Admission charge.

Long Island Maritime Museum

Displays on maritime activities at the turn of the 20th century.
86 West Avenue, West Sayville. Tel: (631) 854 4974; www.limaritime.org. Open: Mon–Sat 10am–4pm, Sun noon–4pm. Admission charge.

Old Bethpage Village Restoration

Pre-Civil War village with costumed guides. Craft demonstrations.

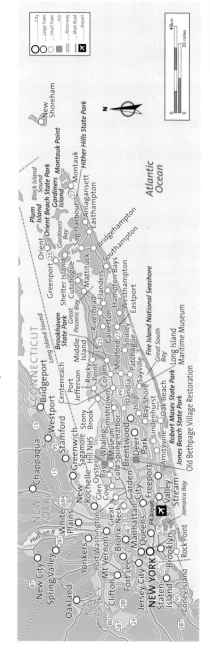

1303 Round Swamp Rd, Old Bethpage.
Tel: (516) 572 8401. Open: Wed–Sun
10am–5pm. Closed: Jan, Feb & holidays,
except Memorial Day, 4 Jul, Labor &
Columbus Days (closed the day after).
Admission charge.

Raynham Hall

The British headquarters during the
Revolution; the 'saltbox' house dates
from 1705, the Gothic wing from 1851.
The gardens reflect colonial and
Victorian design.
20 W Main St, Oyster Bay, Eastern
North Shore. Tel: (516) 922 6808;
www.raynhamhallmuseum.org. Open:
Tue–Sun 1–5pm. Closed: holidays.
Admission charge.

Sagamore Hill National
Historic Site

Teddy Roosevelt's retreat for over
30 years, now a National Historical Site,
has been restored in period style.
20 Sagamore Hill Rd, Oyster Bay,
Eastern North Shore.
Tel: (516) 922 4447. Open: daily
9.30am–5pm. Closed: Thanksgiving,
Christmas Day & New Year's Day.
Admission charge.

Sands Point Park and Preserve

The 'Gold Coast' estate of Daniel and
Harry Guggenheim. A nature centre
provides information on the estate's
wildlife and trails.
Middle Neck Rd, Port Washington.
Tel: (516) 571 7900. Open: May–Oct
Sat–Wed 10am–5pm. Admission charge.

Queens

Most visitors to New York City see Queens before any of the other boroughs, as both John F Kennedy and LaGuardia airports are here. This is New York's biggest borough, and has the second-largest population – over 2 million, including neighbourhoods of Italians, Arabs, Asians, Jews, Hispanics, Greeks and African Americans.

The world spotlight is on Queens when the US Open Tennis Championships take place at Flushing Meadows Park, site of the World Fairs of 1939 and 1964. Queens is also home to the New York Mets baseball team, and two of the USA's most prestigious thoroughbred racetracks, the Aqueduct and Belmont Park.

Whereas many of New York City's residential areas evolved naturally in an era of rapid growth, Queens has seven thoughtfully planned neighbourhoods in which developers allowed for good landscaping and recreational facilities. These neighbourhoods, founded on the garden city concept, have been dubbed the Seven Sisters, the best known being a mock Tudor-style township called Forest Hills Gardens.

Although intended as a low-cost housing project, gentrification elbowed its way in almost before it began, and the well-off – including a strong Jewish community – moved in. Forest Hills is the home of West Side Tennis Club, where the US Open used to be held.

Probably the prettiest of the Sisters is Kew Gardens, with tree-lined streets of well-kept houses in a range of styles. Like Forest Hills, Sunnyside Gardens, in Long Island City, was meant for the working classes when it rose from a swamp in the 1920s. But most lost their homes in the 1930s slump.

Jackson Heights (home of many South Americans), Douglaston, Richmond Hill and the sublimely named Fresh Meadows are the other four Sisters.

The American Museum of the Moving Image

Dedicated to film, television and video, the museum, opened in 1988, gives an insight into production, and has a permanent exhibition on the development of the art form in addition to thousands of items of film memorabilia. Original sets and costumes worn by the stars are displayed, and temporary exhibitions held. Before Hollywood, Astoria was the beating heart of the American film business, and is now making a comeback (*see p146*). The museum is adjacent to the Kaufman Astoria Studios.

35 Ave/37th St, Astoria.
Tel: (718) 784 0077; www.ammi.org.
Open: Tue–Fri 10am–3pm. Admission charge. Subway: Steinway St.

Aqueduct Race Track

This is the largest thoroughbred track in the country, and the only one with its own subway station.

Rockaway Blvd/108th St, Ozone Park.
Tel: (718) 641 4700; www.nyra.com.
Open: Oct–May. Closed: Tue.
Gates open 11am, first race 1pm.
Subway: Aqueduct Race Track.

Belmont Park Race Track

Home of the 'third jewel' in the Triple Crown of thoroughbred racing – the Belmont Stakes. The others are the Kentucky Derby and Preakness. Beautiful grounds with picnic areas and trackside restaurant.

Hempstead Turnpike, Belmont, Long Island. Tel: (516) 488 6000.
Open: May–Jul & late Aug.
Closed: Tue. Rail: Long Island railroad from Manhattan's Penn Station to Queens Village.

Bowne House

One of the city's oldest houses, built in 1661, now a museum illustrating how Quaker John Bowne successfully led the struggle for religious freedom in the 17th century when the Quakers were banned under Dutch rule. Generations

The delightful exterior of John Bowne's house

of Bownes lived at the house until 1947, and their furnishings and ornaments are well displayed.
37–01 Bowne St, Flushing. Tel: (718) 359 0528; www.bownehouse.org. Closed for ongoing restoration. Admission charge. Subway: Main St.

Citi Field

The new home of the New York Mets baseball team, it seats 41,800. (Shea Stadium, the former base of the Mets, was demolished in 2008.)
126th St/Roosevelt Ave, Flushing Meadows-Corona Park.
Tel: (718) 507 8499; www.mets.com. Subway: Shea Stadium.

Flushing Meadows-Corona Park

Site of the 1939 and 1964 New York World Fairs, the park is dominated by the Unisphere, a massive steel globe, and offers boating and a marina, a

The Unisphere at Flushing Meadows

swimming pool, indoor ice-skating, cycling, pitch and putt, a carousel, theatres, the Queens Zoo (*see p123*), a children's farm zoo and the Queens Museum (*see pp122–3*). The park is home to the National Tennis Center where the annual US Open is held.
Jewel/Roosevelt aves, Flushing.
Tel: (718) 760 6565. Subway: Shea Stadium.

Friends' Quaker Meeting House

Built in 1694, it is the borough's oldest place of worship, and is still used.
137–16 Northern Blvd, Flushing.
Tel: (718) 358 9636. Open: Sun 11am–1pm.

Noguchi Museum

Works by the Japanese sculptor Isamu Noguchi, who died in 1988, in the museum and adjoining sculpture garden.
9–01 33rd Rd, Astoria. Tel: (718) 204 7088. Open: Wed–Fri 10am–5pm, Sat & Sun 11am–6pm. Hourly buses leave Asia Society, Park Ave/70th St, Manhattan, every Sun at 30 min past the hour, 12.30–3.30pm. Admission charge.

Jamaica Arts Center

This is a multi-ethnic performing and visual arts centre in an 1898 Italian Renaissance revival building.
16104 Jamaica Ave. Tel: (718) 658 7400. Open: Mon–Fri 9am–8pm, Sat 9am–7.30pm. Free admission. Subway: Jamaica Center (Parsons/Archer).

Jamaica Bay Wildlife Refuge (Gateway National Recreation Area)

Almost as big as Manhattan in area, the refuge is reserved for nature walks, and has 300 species of birds. Visitor permits are available in the grounds.
Crossbay Blvd, Broad Channel.
Tel: (718) 318 4340;
www.brooklynbirdclub.org.
Open: daily dawn–dusk. Free admission.
Subway: Rockaways.

Kingsland Homestead (Queens Historical Society)

Colonial farmhouse built in 1774. Exhibits relating to its history are displayed. The historical society, which provides a do-it-yourself tour leaflet, is headquartered in the house. Outside is a weeping beech tree planted as a cutting from Belgium in 1847, and now officially an historical landmark.
143–35 37th Ave, Flushing.
Tel: (718) 939 0647;
www.queenshistoricalsociety.org.
Open: Tue, Sat & Sun 2.30–4.30pm.
Admission charge. Subway: Main St.

LaGuardia Community College Archives

Interesting for its collection of papers of popular New York City Mayor Fiorello LaGuardia, elected in 1933 during the Depression.
31–10 Thomson Ave.
Tel: (718) 482 5065. Open: Mon–Fri 7.15am–10pm, Sat & Sun 8am–3pm.
Subway: 33rd St.

New York Hall of Science

Science and technology exhibits include Seeing the Light, Realm of the Atom, Hidden Kingdoms and the World of Microbes – topics appealing to children as well as adults. Lots of hands-on exhibits for children.
47–01 111th St, Flushing Meadows.
Tel: (718) 699 0005; www.nyhallsci.org.
Open: Apr–Jun Mon–Thur 9.30am–2pm, Fri 9.30am–5pm, Sat & Sun 10am–6pm; Jul & Aug Mon–Fri 9.30am–5pm, Sat & Sun 10am–6pm; Sept–Mar Tue–Thur 9.30am–2pm, Fri 9.30am–5pm, Sat & Sun 10am–6pm. Admission charge.
Subway: Shea Stadium.

New York State Supreme Court House

This is often used for the shooting of courtroom drama films, as well as real-life trials.
25–10 Court House Square. Subway: 45th St/Court House Square.

P.S.1 MoMA (Project Studio 1)

Cultural centre converted in 1976 from a 19th-century school building,

METHOD IN THE MADNESS

After you have conquered Manhattan's no-nonsense way of numbering its streets and avenues – which does not take long – you come down to earth with a bump when you start exploring Queens. There may be method in the system. If so, it eludes many visitors. If nobody can explain to you how to get to a particular attraction or restaurant, telephone your destination, stating where you are, and ask for exact directions.

The Queensboro Bridge spans the East River and Roosevelt Island

combining art gallery and artists' studios, with occasional exhibitions. *22–25 Jackson Ave at 46th Ave, Long Island City. Tel: (718) 784 2084; www.ps1.org. Open: Thur–Mon noon–6pm. Admission charge. Subway: 45th St/Court House Square.*

Queensboro Bridge

Opened in 1909, this 2,134m (7,000ft)-long bridge across the East River is worth a look. There is a riverside park at the bridge's base.

Queens Botanical Garden

Seasonal floral displays on a 16ha (39-acre) site. The senses are charmed by herb, bee, bird and rose gardens; crab-apple trees and Japanese cherry groves; and a Victorian wedding garden. There is also a plant and gift shop. *43–50 Main St, Flushing. Tel: (718) 886 3800; www.queensbotanical.org.*

Open: Apr–Oct Tue–Fri 8am–6pm, Sat & Sun 8am–7pm; Nov–Mar Tue–Sun 8am–4.30pm. Free admission. Subway: Main St.

Queens County Farm Museum

This restored 200-year-old working farm traces the agricultural history of New York City. Outdoor weekend events (except in winter). *73–50 Little Neck Parkway, Floral Park. Tel: (718) 347 3276; www.queensfarm.org. Open: Mon–Fri 9am–5pm; Sat & Sun 10am–5pm. Free admission.*

Queens Museum

A popular exhibit is the enormous Panorama, a continually updated illuminated model of the five boroughs of New York City, a useful aid to getting your bearings and spotting what you want to see in the full-size version.

Exhibits keep changing. The museum building was the New York Pavilion during the 1939 New York World Fair.

NYC Building, Flushing Meadows. Tel: (718) 592 9700; www.queensmuseum.org. Open: Wed–Sun 10am–6pm. Donation suggested. Subway: Shea Stadium.

Queens Zoo

At the west side of Flushing Meadows-Corona Park, with North American animals in their natural habitats and the feel of a miniature National Park.

Jewel/Roosevelt aves, Flushing. Tel: (718) 271 1500; www.queenszoo.com. Open: summer weekdays 10am–5pm, weekends & holidays 10am–5.30pm, winter daily 10am–4.30pm. Admission charge. Subway: Shea Stadium.

The Rockaways

Nearly 16km (10 miles) of beaches on a spit of land in the Atlantic Ocean,

AROUND QUEENS

Long Island City is an industrial and commercial area of Queens; there used to be a good ferry connection with Manhattan. Development began early in the 19th century. Prosperous business people built gracious homes along the frontage of the East River in Vernon Boulevard.

Hunterspoint Historic District, 45th Avenue, provides a pleasant stroll among well-maintained rowhouses with quaint verandas. Around a small park at 21st Street are warehouses providing studio space for artists at much lower rents than those demanded on Manhattan.

with Jacob Riis Park at the western end. Take the subway to Rockaway Park Beach.

St Demetrius Cathedral

The cathedral has the biggest Greek Orthodox congregation outside Greece.

30–11 30th Drive, Astoria. Subway: Broadway.

The industrial side of Queens, Long Island City

New Amsterdam

Once upon a time, the tallest building in New York was a two-storey windmill. That was in 1664 when Dutch rule of the place, then called Nieuw Amsterdam, was drawing to a close. In 1624, 30 families had sailed from Holland to settle on Nut Island – now known as Governor's Island – in New York Harbor. The settlement grew rapidly.

In 1626, the governor, Peter Minuit, stood at Old Fort Amsterdam – later to become the site of the US Customs House at Bowling Green – to acquire Manhattan Island from a party of Algonquin Indians for $24-worth of baubles, beads and brightly coloured cloth. Governor Minuit reckoned he had a great bargain, and since it was not theirs to sell, the Algonquins, too, were happy with the arrangement.

A year earlier, in 1625, the Dutch had formed the fur trading post of

Peter Minuit buys Manhattan for $24-worth of trinkets

The Dutch arrive on Staten Island

Nieuw Amsterdam. Beaver fur was the mainstay of the enterprise, and the beaver still features on the city's seal. The Dutch built a wall from the East River to the Hudson River in 1653 – Wall Street follows its line – to protect their colony from Indians and from British trade competitors.

But, in 1664, the British took the city without a fight (Dutch governor Peter Stuyvesant reluctantly surrendered the city) and named it after the Duke of York, the brother of King Charles II. Lower Manhattan was like a ping-pong ball for a time. The Dutch recaptured it in 1673, calling it New Orange, and the British regained control the following year, remaining in charge until the Revolutionary War ended in 1783, with the Americans gaining independence. George Washington was sworn in as the first president at Federal Hall in New York.

Staten Island

Until the Verrazano-Narrows Bridge opened in 1964, linking it with Brooklyn, Staten Island was the poor relation of New York City. It was a small fishing and farming community, which tended to keep itself to itself.

Once the bridge went up, neighbours looked covetously at the property prices in Staten Island, bought land, set up desirable residences and commuted. Enough of the woodland has been retained to put the smallest borough on the tourist trail.

Staten Island may be the least visited of the city's boroughs, but for those seeking quiet refuge or sights off the beaten track it is certainly worth a visit.

Staten Island has a zoo, a restoration project, a botanical garden, a cultural centre and a handful of museums – all worthy attractions. Most visitors, however, are attracted by the idea of a good view of New York Harbor, Ellis Island and the Statue of Liberty, which they can get at no extra charge on the Staten Island Ferry. They disembark at Bay Street Landing in the town of St George.

Those interested in history will find time well spent on Staten Island. The attractions are somewhat spread out, but bus rides to most areas provide an opportunity to enjoy the scenery. After a few days in Manhattan, where, at best, gulls and pigeons represent the wildlife, non-city dwellers will be relieved to find rural surroundings. Sports facilities include golf, hiking, tennis and – in winter – skiing and sledging.

Alice Austen House Museum and Garden

Less than 3km (2 miles) south of Bay Street Landing is the Dutch-style Victorian cottage overlooking New York Harbor where the renowned photographer Alice Austen spent most of her life. She was given her first camera at the age of 10. The pictures she took until her death in her mid-80s in 1952 provide a wonderful record of Staten Island and its people. A selection is on view at the restored cottage. There is a gift shop.
2 Hylan Blvd. Tel: (718) 816 4506; www.aliceausten.org. Open: Thur–Sun noon–5pm. Donations welcome. Bus: S51 from Bay St.

OYSTERS GALORE

Oyster farming was an important industry off Staten Island's south shore in the early 19th century. Descendants of free black people from Maryland, brought in to work in the industry, still live on the island.

The Alice Austen House, pictured in 1892

Barrett Park and Cloves Lake Park

Visitors will find a bridle path, ice skating rink, model boating pond and fishing facilities, together with the Staten Island Zoo, all about 1.6km (1 mile) southwest of Snug Harbor. *1150 Clove Rd, West Brighton.*

Clay Pit Ponds Park

This is the only state park on the island. Horses can be hired from V & S Stables. *83 Nielson Ave, Staten Island. Tel: (718) 967 1976.*

Conference House

A meeting took place here in 1776 with the specific aim of preventing the Revolution. Benjamin Franklin met with John Adams, Edward Rutledge and the British admiral Lord Howe, but, as history records, the meeting failed. The stone manor house was built in 1675. *298 Satterlee St, far southwest of the island. Tel: (718) 984 6046; www.conferencehouse.org. Open: Apr–mid-Dec Fri–Sun 1–4pm. Admission charge.*

Council on the Arts and Humanities for Staten Island

This organisation promotes all aspects of the island's diverse cultural life – music, theatre, dance, art and the humanities. It issues a free guide to cultural events and runs a tourist and cultural information centre across the water in the South Ferry Passenger Terminal, Manhattan. *Snug Harbor Cultural Center, 1000 Richmond Terrace. Tel: (718) 447 3329; www.statenislandarts.org. Open: Mon–Fri 9am–5pm.*

Garibaldi-Meucci Museum

Who invented the telephone? Antonio Meucci's claim to have done so before

Historic Richmondtown regularly recreates Staten Island's past

Alexander Graham Bell is well documented at this museum, which has mid-19th-century memorabilia and letters and photographs illustrating the life of Italian revolutionary Giuseppe Garibaldi, who spent some time in the borough. The museum is in a restored Federal farmhouse.
420 Tompkins Ave, Rosebank. Tel: (718) 442 1608; www.garibaldimeuccimuseum.org. Open: Tue–Sun 1–5pm. Admission charge.

Gateway National Recreation Area

Beaches and shoreland at the east of the island, extending over 10,522ha (26,000 acres), with occasional special events. Sports facilities include tennis, volleyball, basketball, baseball and football. Managed by the National Parks Service.
Great Kills Park, New Dorp. Open: daily sunrise–sunset. Free admission.

The Green Belt

A 1,012ha (2,500-acre) expanse of swamp and freshwater ponds formed by an Ice Age glacier, with woodlands, grassland and wetlands, and trails to follow. Animals and birds in their natural habitats. High Rock Park Conservation Center, a popular hiking area, is within the Green Belt. Amenities include a visitor centre, gallery and gift shop. Guided and self-guided tours are available.
200 Nevada Ave/Rockland Ave. Tel: (718) 667 2165; www.sigreenbelt.org. Open: Mon–Fri 9am–5pm. Free admission.

Jacques Marchais Center of Tibetan Art

A reproduction Buddhist monastery, situated on a steep hillside, housing the western hemisphere's biggest collection of Tibetan artworks, musical instruments, ornaments, costumes, bronze images and ritual objects. Educational programmes are on offer. Phone for the date of the Harvest Festival celebrated by monks at the centre in the first half of October, when Tibetan foods and craft works are on sale. Jacques Marchais was an arts dealer.

338 Lighthouse Ave, Staten Island.
Tel: (718) 987 3500;
www.tibetanmuseum.org. Open:
Wed–Sun 1–5pm. Admission charge.
Bus: S74 from ferry terminal.

Museum of the Staten Island Institute of Arts and Sciences

About 1.6km (1 mile) east of Snug Harbor, the museum has displays of natural history and fine arts.

A 1930s postcard from the Staten Island Museum Collection

75 Stuyvesant Place, St George.
Tel: (718) 727 1135;
www.statenislandmuseum.org. Open:
Sun–Fri noon–5pm, Sat 10am–5pm.
Admission charge.

Richmondtown Restoration

Founded in the late 17th century, Richmondtown was the county seat of the island, and is now Staten Island Historical Society's ongoing labour of love. There are 26 historic buildings on a site of nearly 40ha (100 acres). Some of the buildings have been brought from elsewhere on Staten Island and reconstructed, blending in with the original 18th-century buildings. The 1695 Voorlezer's House is the oldest standing elementary school in the USA. There is a general store, plenty of old Dutch colonial architecture and the 1740 Guyon-Lake Tyson House on Staten Island's first permanent settlement, dating back to 1685. The visitor centre is housed in the 19th-century Greek Revival courthouse. The historic museum traces 300 years of Staten Island life. Toys, furniture, tools, china and other domestic and agricultural items of past centuries are exhibited, with a vast collection of photographs, including many works of Alice Austen, a local recorder of events and people. The restored village is frequently the scene of special events, including flea markets, an Easter egg hunt, a Yankee Pedlar day, a display of Staten Island samplers, an antiques and craft market, a Civil War encampment weekend and an Independence Day ice-cream social. Craftspeople and tradespeople in costume use the techniques of long ago. The village includes a museum of childhood, with antique dolls and toys and small-scale furniture.

441 Clarke Ave at Arthur Kill/Amboy rds. Tel: (718) 351 1611; www.historicrichmondtown.org. Open: Wed–Sun 1–5pm. Guided tours Wed–Fri 2.30pm, Sat & Sun 2pm, 3.30pm, otherwise self-guided tour. Admission charge. Bus: S74 Richmond Road from ferry terminal.

Snug Harbor Cultural Center

National Historic District of American Architecture on 83 acres (34ha) of parkland. Originally a farm overlooking a waterway that runs into Upper New York Bay, it became a 'snug harbor' for retired sailors in 1831.

There are several Greek Revival temple-like buildings with columns, one of which still reflects its nautical connections in the pictures and ornaments in its main hall. Today, there are displays of contemporary art and sculpture, and musical performances and indoor concerts are held in the Veterans' Memorial Hall, the former chapel. Outdoor concerts and recitals are given in summer by such high-calibre players as the New York Philharmonic and the Metropolitan Opera. Guided tours are given on weekend afternoons.

1000 Richmond Terrace.

ANTIQUE HAVEN

Close to the ferry terminal at Staten Island is St George's, where a number of shops, including a group in the Edgewater Hall Antiques Center, a converted bank building, sell furniture, artefacts and adornments of days gone by.

Tel: (718) 448 2500; www.snug-harbor.org. Open: daily 8am–dusk. Charge for group tours. Trolley service between ferry terminal and Snug Harbor, or S40 bus.

Staten Island Botanical Garden

On the Snug Harbor complex, the 32ha (80-acre) site includes a scented garden for the blind, a perennial garden, 4ha (10 acres) of natural marsh habitat, specimen trees, ponds, a greenhouse, a bonsai collection and beds of floral displays. On Sunday afternoons you can take a guided tree walk.

914 Richmond Terrace/Snug Harbor Rd. Tel: (718) 273 8200; www.snug-harbor.org. Open: daily dawn–dusk. Free admission.

Staten Island Children's Museum

An imaginative museum, it has some revolving exhibitions in which children can participate, learning about natural history and aspects of everyday life, such as the television. Exhibitions are held in the grounds in the Newhouse Center for Contemporary Art.

*1000 Richmond Terrace/
Snug Harbor Rd. Tel: (718) 273 2060;
www.statenislandkids.org.
Museum open: Tue–Sun noon–5pm on
school days, 10am–5pm on holidays.
Admission charge.
Newhouse Center open: Tue–Sun
10am–5pm. Donation suggested.*

Staten Island Zoo

With the accent on quality rather
than quantity, the zoo is renowned
for having one of the world's finest
reptile collections. A children's zoo
is incorporated.
*Barrett Park, 614 Broadway.
Tel: (718) 442 3100/3174;
www.statenislandzoo.org. Open: daily
10am–4.45pm. Admission charge.*

Verrazano-Narrows Bridge

Opened in 1964, with twin towers the
height of a 70-storey building

supporting the 1,298m (4,260ft)
suspension span, this bridge links
Staten Island and Brooklyn. It was the
world's longest suspension bridge until
one was built over the River Humber
in the United Kingdom. It was
constructed by Othmar Ammann,
a man already responsible for
overseeing the building of eight
other New York bridges. More than
30,000 runners cross it in the
New York Marathon.

William T Davis Wildlife Refuge

Some 105ha (260 acres) of woodland,
fields, tidal marsh and freshwater
wetlands. Plants, animals, birds and
reptiles that may be encountered
are indicated on the trails. Tours can
be arranged.
*Travis/Richmond aves, New Springville.
Tel: (718) 667 2165. Open: daily
dawn–dusk. Free admission.*

Staten Island Children's Museum

Getting away from it all

Even in New York there comes a time when visitors yearn for a change of pace and scene. It happens to New Yorkers themselves, who are great weekenders. There are many interesting and exciting things to see and do within easy reach, and the choice widens considerably for those who can take a break of two or three days.

OPEN SPACES

New York has no shortage of open space among all those cubic kilometres of glass and concrete. More than 1,500 parks and playgrounds alone cover a total of 10,522ha (26,000 acres).

Beaches

There are several good beaches close to Manhattan. Most can be reached by subway, but some get very crowded on summer weekends. Quieter coastal areas – with better beaches – are to be found further east on Long Island.

Brooklyn's beaches can all be reached by the subway's D train, so naturally they pull in the crowds. **Brighton Beach**, at the eastern end of Coney Island (which is actually a peninsula), is in the area known as Little Odessa because so many of its residents are Russian immigrants.

Coney Island Beach is the archetypal seaside resort, brash and popular, with amusement arcades and fairground rides. Once fashionable, it first attracted attention in the 1840s. In recent years, however, it has declined, although the standard of its traditional ethnic snacks remains high.

Smaller than either of the two above beaches, **Manhattan Beach** is on the same stretch of Coney Island coast, but is a little more upmarket, and mainly attracts local residents.

The best of the beaches close to Manhattan – and therefore the most popular – is **Rockaway Beach**, 12km (7½ miles) of sand and surf on a spit of land south of Jamaica Bay. Subway trains A and C stop at stations along the beach. To the west is **Jacob Riis Park**, which has good sandy beaches, and is popular with the gay community.

Further east on Long Island, the white sands of **Long Beach** and **Jones Beach State Park** entice New Yorkers beyond the metropolitan boundary. Both can be reached by train from Manhattan's Penn Station to Freeport, where there is a bus connection.

Botanical gardens

Covering an area of 21ha (52 acres), **Brooklyn Botanic Garden** (*see p108*) is an intimate retreat next door to the Brooklyn Museum. Its main feature is an enchanting Japanese Garden, and there are fragrance, rose and herb gardens, as well as a conservatory with tropical, desert and temperate pavilions. **New York Botanical Garden** in the Bronx covers 101ha (250 acres) alongside the Bronx River Gorge. Inspired by London's Kew Gardens, it includes a 16ha (40-acre) forest among its attractions (*see p103*). **Staten Island Botanical Garden** is on 32ha (80 acres) at Snug Harbor, and features trees, ponds and a natural marsh habitat (*see p130*).

Cemeteries

A cemetery might be the last place you would expect to visit on holiday, but two in New York are certainly worth the visit. Both have illustrious and notorious names on elaborate tombs.

At Brooklyn's **Greenwood Cemetery**, you can take a guided tour of its 193ha (478 acres). Among its incumbents are members of the Steinway piano family

Getting away from it all

Coney Island's funfair is popular with families

in a 119-room mausoleum. **Woodlawn Cemetery**, North Bronx, is the last resting place for a number of famous names, among them the jazz wizard Duke Ellington.

Parks

Fort Tryon and **Inwood Parks**, at the northern end of Manhattan, offer stunning views of the Hudson River and New Jersey shore. Landscaped by Frederick Law Olmsted, the Central Park designer, Fort Tryon encompasses **The Cloisters** (*see pp82–3*), which houses the Metropolitan Museum of Art medieval collection. **Inwood**, where Indian cave dwellers once lived, contains the Dyckman House, a restored 18th-century Dutch farmhouse.

Kissena Park in southwest Flushing, Queens, has walking trails through its 95ha (235 acres) of protected forest and marshland. **Pelham Bay Park**, on the northeast edge of the Bronx overlooking Long Island Sound, is the city's largest, covering more than 809ha (2,000 acres). It was purchased from the Indians by Thomas Pell in 1654, and today lists canoeing, cycling, horse riding and 1.6km (1 mile) of beach among its amenities. In Brooklyn, **Prospect Park** (*see p115*) has a zoo, music grove, skating rink and boating lakes in 213ha (526 acres).

River trips

Manhattan's most obvious open space is the water that surrounds it: a 56km

A red panda at the Prospect Park zoo, Brooklyn

(35-mile) trip lasting three hours if the island is circumnavigated. Circle Line offers year-round trips up to 13 times a day from its own plaza at the Hudson River end of 42nd Street. A faster alternative is The Beast Speed Boat, a 30-minute, 72kph (45mph) race through New York Harbor (May–October only). There is also a two-hour evening cruise of New York Harbor and Lower Manhattan. Metropolitan Cruise Line, Spirit of New York and World Yacht offer luncheon and dinner cruises around Manhattan. (*See p184 for more information.*)

Wildlife

Central Park after dark and the subway's seedier sections are not the only places to observe life in the wild in New York. Gentler, more natural aspects can be viewed – often unexpectedly – in many locations.

Birdwatchers will have a rewarding time in Central and other parks. Large tracts of seashore, especially on **Long Island**, offer sanctuary to many varieties of wildfowl and seabirds. Whale-watching tours operate from Montauk, at the eastern tip of Long Island.

Jamaica Bay Wildlife Refuge straddles the southern boundaries of Brooklyn and Queens, and lies beneath the JFK Airport flight path. Nevertheless, some 300 species of birds and small mammals manage to live there undisturbed, especially egrets and herons, and an abundance of waders and other shorebirds. Covering more than 3,642ha (9,000 acres) of land and water, the refuge is almost as big as Manhattan (*see p121*).

To the east, **Jones Beach State Park**, **Lawrence Marsh**, **Orient Beach State Park** and **Moriches Bay** present wonderful opportunities for beachcombers to seek out clams and crabs, shells and sand dollars, shoreline vegetation and yet more birds. Long Island's rural terrain – pastures and woodland – is the habitat of such species as the blue jay, the colourful American goldfinch, catbirds and mockingbirds, and for mammals, including chipmunks and grey squirrels.

Naturalists will find it worthwhile taking a break in New Jersey. **Great Swamp National Wildlife Refuge**, a few kilometres west of Newark, has both marsh and woodland habitats harbouring warblers, flycatchers, woodpeckers, rails, ducks and herons. **Brigantine National Wildlife Refuge**, near Atlantic City, has egrets, herons and ibises in a labyrinth of freshwater pools and salt marshes. Further south, **Cape May** is renowned for its autumn migrations of warblers, vireos and birds of prey.

The city's waterways offer an alternative view of the skyline

OUTER REACHES

A break from the city of two or three days can bring rich rewards. The eastern extremity of Long Island is not much more than 201km (125 miles) from Manhattan, and there is much to be seen in the neighbouring states of Connecticut and New Jersey. New York State's attractions are legion and accessible – even Niagara Falls, on the Canadian border, is barely an hour's flight away.

Connecticut
Yale University

An hour and three-quarters' rail journey from New York's Grand Central Station, by Amtrak or Metro-North, leads to New Haven, Connecticut, home of the Ivy League Yale University. Founded in 1701, Yale now has 13,000 students.

The oldest building on the campus, Connecticut Hall, is a Georgian structure of 1752, now the Department of Philosophy. Other old buildings serve as dormitories and classrooms.

Visitors may wander the campus on their own (maps available from the information office, from where the guided tours also leave).
Phelps Gate, College Street.
www.yale.edu/visitor.
Tours: Mon–Fri 10.30am & 2pm,
Sat & Sun 1.30pm.

Long Island

Shaped like a squid on the move, Long Island has rural landscapes and sand-fringed shores that soon leave the gritty metropolis behind.

The island's North Shore is more rugged, with wooded headlands, coves and cliffs, and the mansions that cause its western section to be known as the Gold Coast. Many of the lavish homes were built in the Roaring 20s. The town of Great Neck is the West Egg of F Scott Fitzgerald's novel *The Great Gatsby*.

The South Shore is best known for its beaches, Jones Beach, Oak Beach and Fire Island, favoured by the gay community. There are few places of note in the west of the island, except perhaps Amityville whose haunted house still broods on a hill in the town.

For a real break, it is best to slog on eastwards, where the island divides into North Fork and South Fork. North Fork is wilder, with fewer tourists. Its few towns have a distinctly New England character. Orient Point has a state park and the ferry connects it to New London, Connecticut.

South Fork is best known for The Hamptons – Westhampton, Hampton Bays, Southampton, Bridgehampton and Easthampton – a group of small, suave towns with wealthy residents. North of The Hamptons, historic Sag Harbor is a former whaling port with the Whalers' Presbyterian Church, a whalers' museum and graves in the Oakland cemetery. To the east, wind-blown Montauk huddles among the sand dunes.
Sag Harbor Whaling and Historical Museum. 200 Main St, Long Island.

Tel: (631) 725 0770;
www.sagharborwhalingmuseum.org.
Open: May–Oct Mon–Sat 10am–5pm,
Sun 1–5pm. Admission charge.

New York State

Travelling north, it is not long before you reach the beautiful countryside of the Hudson Valley. Tarrytown, barely 32km (20 miles) from midtown Manhattan, was the village in Washington Irving's *The Legend of Sleepy Hollow*. Irving himself lived at nearby Sunnyside, a Dutch farmhouse estate now open to the public and well worth a visit. Also in Tarrytown is Lyndhurst, a Gothic Revival mansion, and Philipsburg Manor and Mill, an authentically restored estate that was built by Dutch settlers in the early 17th century. Also accessible from Tarrytown, in Kykuit, is the Rockefeller Mansion, open to the public.

West of the river, and still a mere 64km (40 miles) from Manhattan, is Bear Mountain State Park, with hiking trails and boat rentals. Just north of here is the United States Military Academy at West Point, a cradle of American military leaders since 1802. West Point has a visitor information centre, a museum and lots of boisterous parade activity.

Hudson Valley destinations can be reached by bus, train (commuter service from Grand Central Station), Day Line Ferry services or by car.
Sunnyside. West Sunnyside Lane, Tarrytown. Tel: (914) 591 8763.
Open: Apr–Oct Wed–Mon 10am–5pm; Oct–Dec Wed–Mon 10am–4pm; Nov Sat & Sun 10am–4pm. Closed: holidays. Admission charge.
Rockefeller Mansion. Tel: (914) 631 9491). Open: May–Nov daily 10am–3pm. Closed: Tue. Admission charge. Tours of the estate begin at Philipsbury Manor on Route 9 in Sleepy Hollow.
US Military Academy. West Point, NY. Tel: (845) 938 2638; www.usma.edu. Grounds and Military Museum open: daily 10.30am–4.15pm. Information Center open: daily 9am–4.45pm. Closed: Thanksgiving, Christmas and New Year's Day.

A typical Victorian house in Sea Cliff, Long Island

Shopping

World-famous for its magnificent department stores, New York is also a discount shopper's delight. Designer-label clothes from fashion's top names are offered in the Orchard Street area, in the Lower East Side, at a fraction of big-store prices. It is open on Sundays, but closed on Friday afternoons and Saturdays. For electronic goods at discount prices, try Canal Street and Essex Street downtown. In short, New York is one of the world's great shopping cities.

WHERE AND WHAT TO BUY

Speciality shops, boutiques and exclusive outlets make for interesting browsing and buying. Try Pier 17 at South Street Seaport, Rockefeller Center, World Financial Center and the shops at Columbus Circle Time Warner Center.

New York's many ethnic communities sell handcrafted gifts and other goods in all five boroughs. The major shopping area is midtown Manhattan.

LOWER MANHATTAN
Antiques
Hyde Park Antiques
The shop stocks period furniture dating back to the early 1700s.
836 Broadway/13th St. Tel: (212) 477 0033; www. hydeparkantiques.com

Books
Biography Bookshop
An extensive range of biographies from around the world.
400 Bleecker/11th St. Tel: (212) 807 8655.

St Mark's Bookshop
A variety of books for serious reading.
31 3rd Ave/9th St. Tel: (212) 260 7853; www. stmarksbookshop.com

Clothing
Abercrombie & Fitch
Casual, inexpensive and an all-American appeal.
199 Water St at South Street Seaport. Tel: (212) 809 9000; www.abercrombie.com

Banana Republic
Classic clothing.
550 Broadway/Prince St. Tel: (212) 925 0308; www.bananarepublic.com

Gifts
Blue Nile
An uptown boutique for soaps, shampoos, room sprays and candles.
324 Bleecker St, near 7th Ave. Tel: (646) 336 1118.

Movie Star News
Posters galore in a former carriage house.
134 W 18th St, near 7th Ave. Tel: (212) 620 8160; www.moviestarnews.com

Records
Bleecker Bob's
Rock, reggae and punk golden oldies.
118 W 3rd St/McDougal. Tel: (212) 475 9677.

Disc-O-Rama
Discounted music.
44 W 8th St;
Tel: (212) 477 9410;
www.discorama.com

Kim's Video & Music
Extensive collection of
CDs and vinyl, imports
and films.
124 1st Ave.
Tel: (212) 533 7390;
www.mondokims.com

Toys

Dinosaur Hill Toy Store
Delightful handmade
toys, clothes, games and
gifts for infants, children
and adults.
306 East 9th St
(1st/2nd aves).
Tel: (212) 473 5850;
www.dinosaurhill.com

The Scholastic Store
A massive children's
bookshop that also sells
toys, games, puzzles and
videos.
557 Broadway, near
Prince St.
Tel: (212) 343 6166;
www.store.scholastic.com

Torly Kid
Torly Kid, formerly
Babylicious, specialises in
items for kids aged 9–12.
51 Hudson St/Thomas St.
Tel: (212) 406 7440;
www.torlykid.com

MIDTOWN MANHATTAN

Antiques

Howard Kaplan Designs.
240 East 60th St
(2nd/3rd aves).
Tel: (646) 443 7170; www.
howardkaplandesigns.com

Manhattan Art and Antiques Center
More than 100 antiques
stores and galleries.
1050 2nd Ave/56th St.
Tel: (212) 355 4400;
www.the-maac.com

The Show Place
135 antique dealers in a
three-storey building.
40 W 25th St
(Broadway/Ave of the
Americas).
Tel: (212) 633 6063;
www.nyshowplace.com

Books

Asia Society Bookstore and Gift Shop
Asian prints, art books,
toys and jewellery.
725 Park Ave.
Tel: (212) 327-9217;
www.asiastore.org

Barnes & Noble
Balconies, nooks and
crannies and thousands
of books. Scattered across
the city. *555 5th Ave.*
Tel: (212) 697 3048;
www.barnesandnoble.com

Strand Book Store
Selling new, used and
rare books, the Strand
has been an institution in
the city since 1927.
828 Broadway.
Tel: (212) 473-1452;
www.strandbooks.com

Clothing

Brooks Brothers
A high-class menswear
establishment, various
locations.
346 Madison Ave/44th St.
Tel: (212) 682 8800;
www.brooksbrothers.com

Gucci
The name says it all. This
is the flagship store.
725 5th Ave. Tel: (212)
826 2600; www.gucci.com

H & M
A great place for bargain
hunters. A popular haunt
for men's and women's
fashion.
111 5th Ave at 18th St.
Tel: (212) 539 1741;
www.hm.com

Cameras/electronics

42nd Street Photo
Negotiable discounts on
goods sold by eager sales
assistants.
378 5th Ave, near 35th St.
Tel: (212) 594 6565;
www.42photo.com

B&H Photo Video

This is a fun store to visit – even if you aren't in the market for camera equipment.
420 9th Ave.
Tel: (212) 444-6708;
www.bhphotovideo.com

Willoughby's

High reputation for service at this camera and accessory store.
298 5th Ave.
Tel: (212) 564 1600;
www.willoughbys.com

Department stores

Barney's New York

Fragrances, jewellery and labels from across the globe.
660 Madison Ave.
Tel: (212) 826 8900;
www.barneys.com

Bergdorf Goodman

Genteel atmosphere, beautiful things.
754 5th Ave
(57th/58th sts).
Tel: (212) 753 7300; www.
bergdorfgoodman.com

Bloomingdales

A busy store, with racks crammed full and sometimes great mark-downs on designer goods.
1000 3rd Ave/59th St.
Tel: (212) 705 2000;
www.bloomingdales.com

Macy's

Herald Square's anchor, with creative window displays that draw crowds all year long.
151 W 34th St.
Tel: (212) 695 4400;
www.macys.com

Manhattan Mall

Eight floors of speciality shops and Stern's – fashions for all, household goods, gifts, toys and a food floor.
100 W 33rd St/6th Ave.
Tel: (212) 465 0500; www.
manhattanmallny.com

Saks Fifth Avenue

Gracious living personified at this store, founded in the 1920s.
611 5th Ave/50th St.
Tel: (212) 753 4000;
www.saksfifthavenue.com

Gifts

Bath & Body Works

High-quality, scented bath products.
304 Park Ave.
Tel: (212) 674 7385; www.
bathandbodyworks.com

Steuben

Fine crystal made at the Corning Glass Center in New York State.
667 Madison Ave/61st St.
Tel: (212) 752 1441;
www.steuben.com

Jewellery

Tiffany's

Not everything costs the earth. Pretty things, at affordable prices too.
727 5th Ave/57th St.
Tel: (212) 755 8000;
www.tiffany.com

Music

Colony Record & Radio Center

CDs, sheet music and karaoke supplies.
1619 Broadway.
Tel: (212) 265 2020;
www.colonymusic.com

Toys

The Disney Store

Classic Mickey memorabilia and more.
210 W 42nd St.
Tel: (212) 221 0430.

FAO Schwarz

The ultimate toy emporium, with friendly staff in fancy costume.
767 5th Ave/58th St.
Tel: (212) 644 9400;
www.fao.com

Kidding Around

Inviting store with everything from beautiful dolls to old-fashioned wooden rocking horses.
60 W 15th St (8th/9th aves). Tel: (212) 645 6337;
www.kiddingaround.us

Toys 'R' Us
Several floors of
everything for children
dominated by a full-sized
indoor Ferris wheel.
1514 Broadway, Times Sq.
Tel: (646) 366 8800;
www.toysrus.com

UPPER MANHATTAN
Antiques
Alexander's Antiques
Arts and antiques.
1050 2nd Ave.
Tel: (212) 935 9386;
www.alexantiques.com
Florian Papp
An Upper East Side
institution; fine crafts.
962 Madison Ave
(75th/76th sts).
Tel: (212) 288 6770;
www.florianpapp.com

Books
Barnes & Noble
Cut-price books.
150 E 86th St/Lexington
Ave. Tel: (212) 369 2180;
www.barnesandnoble.com
**Westside Rare and Used
Books**
Right across from
Zabar's, this is the place
to buy, sell and trade new
and used books.
2246 Broadway/81st St.
Tel: (212) 362 0706;
www.westsiderbooks.com

Clothing
Ann Taylor
Very popular for chic
women's clothing.
645 Madison Ave.
Tel: (212) 832 9114;
www.anntaylor.com
Barneys New York
Department store for
designer clothing.
660 Madison Ave.
Tel: (212) 826 8900;
www.barneys.com
Gap
Several locations across
the city. Fabulous jeans,
khakis and trendy wear.
2373 Broadway/86th St.
Tel: (212) 873 1244;
www.gap.com
Givenchy
Classically elegant wear.
710 Madison Ave/63rd St.
Tel: (212) 688 4338;
www.givenchy.com

Ethnic shopping
Chinese Porcelain Co
Exquisite souvenirs.
475 Park Ave.
Tel: (212) 838 7744; www.
chineseporcelainco.com
Himalayan Crafts
Wood- and stone-carved
items, textiles, herbs and
incense.
2007 Broadway.
Tel: (212) 787 8500;
www.himalayancraft.com

Things Japanese
Ceramics, scrolls and
other elegant goods.
800 Lexington Ave.
Tel: (212) 371 4661;
www.thingsjapanese.com

Gifts
**The Metropolitan
Museum of Art Shop**
Terrific reproductions.
1000 5th Ave/82nd St.
Tel: (212) 879 5500; www.
metmuseum.org/store

Records
Tower Records
Chain record store.
725 5th Ave.
Tel: (212) 838 8110.
Westsider Records
A large selection of vinyl
records, CDs and films
(VHS and DVD).
233 W 72nd St/Broadway.
Tel: (212) 874 1588;
www.westsiderbooks.com

Toys
Mary Arnold Toys
From dolls and blocks to
the most technologically
advanced games there
are, Mary Arnold Toys
has it all.
1010 Lexington Ave
(72nd/73rd sts).
Tel: (212) 744 8510;
www.maryarnoldtoys.com

Entertainment

More than anywhere else on earth, New York is entertainment. Ballet, classical music, opera; big-cast musicals, jazz, rock; theatre and film; cabaret, discos, piano bars – it is all here, alive and kicking, and it is absolutely the best in the world.

Current listings are given in the *New York Times*, *Village Voice*, *Village Times*, *Time Out New York* (*TONY*) and the *New Yorker*. It's well worth checking details on availability of both regular and discounted tickets from: Telecharge (*tel: (212) 239 6200*) and Ticketmaster (*tel: (212) 307 7171*). Internet events guides include: *www.nycgo.com; www.new.york.eventguide.com; www.broadwayleague.com* (*also see p180*).

Ballet and dance
Dance Theatre of Harlem
466 W 152nd St. Tel: (212) 690 2800; www.dancetheatreofharlem.com. Subway: 157th St/ Broadway.
Juilliard School
60 Lincoln Center Plaza/W 65th St. Tel: (212) 769 7406; www.juilliard.edu
Merce Cunningham Studio
55 Bethune St. Tel: (212) 255 8240; www.merce.org

LUNCHTIME CONCERTS
There are many, usually free, lunchtime performances given at an increasing number of locations throughout the city.
Among these, the best known are the **Citicorp Center Marketplace** (*54th Street/Lexington Avenue*) and the **Continental Insurance Atrium** (*180 Maiden Lane*). Also downtown, **Trinity Church** (*Broadway/Wall Street*) presents free concerts of mostly classical music on Thursdays at 1pm. Similar events take place at 12.10pm on Mondays and Thursdays in **St Paul's Chapel** (*Fulton Street/Broadway*).

Concerts and opera
Alice Tully Hall
Intimate, yet seating close to 1,100, with acoustics said to be near-perfect, this is an ideal location for performances by the Lincoln Center Chamber Music Society, soloists and concert groups. *Lincoln Center, W 62nd St, Broadway. Tel: (212) 875 5000; www.new.lincolncenter.org*
Avery Fisher Hall
Another Lincoln Center hall, it seats 2,740, and is home of the New York

Philharmonic. During the summer its Mostly Mozart Festival features artists of international stature performing works by contemporary composers as well as the classical greats.

North side of Main Plaza, Lincoln Center.
Tel: (212) 875 5709; www.nyphil.org

Bargemusic

A floating location for chamber music and jazz, in the shadow of Brooklyn Bridge.

Fulton Ferry Landing, Brooklyn Heights.
Tel: (718) 624 2083;
www.bargemusic.org

Brooklyn Academy of Music

Respected for its musical experimentation, and home of the Brooklyn Philharmonic, the Brooklyn Academy of Music (BAM) has entered into a partnership with the Metropolitan Opera to mount innovative opera productions and commission new works.

30 Lafayette Ave, Brooklyn.
Tel: (718) 636 4100; www.bam.org

Carnegie Hall

World-famous for more than a century – this was where Paderewski was

Jazz in the streets

acclaimed in 1891, Leonard Bernstein in 1943 and the Beatles in 1963. One of the world's premier concert venues, Carnegie Hall is an institution for the whole range of musical experience.
154 W 57th St/7th Ave.
Tel: (212) 247 7800;
www.carnegiehall.org

Grace Rainey Rogers Auditorium

Within the Metropolitan Museum of Art, this auditorium hosts classical music by acclaimed artists.
1000 5th Ave/82nd St.
Tel: (212) 570 3949;
www.metmuseum.org

Metropolitan Opera

Stunning performances with superstar singers in the most elegant of surroundings at the Lincoln Center. The season runs from September to April.
Lincoln Center.
Tel: (212) 362 6000; www.metopera.org

New York City Opera

In residence at the Lincoln Center's New York State Theater, the company performs popular musicals (*South Pacific, The Sound of Music,* etc.), as well as a range of full-blown operas.
20 Lincoln Center. Tel: (212) 870 5570;
www.nycopera.com

Jazz, blues and folk

Birdland

Live jazz nightly, with big names appearing at weekends.
315 W 44th St. Tel: (212) 581 3080;
www.birdlandjazz.com

GREAT OUTDOORS

During the summer, the city's parks are alive with the sound of music. Even the famous Metropolitan Opera and the ever-popular New York Philharmonic go alfresco, and performances are free.

In August, the Out of Doors festival takes to the **Lincoln Center Plaza** (*tel: (212) 360 1333*) for events in city parks. (*Tel: (212) 877 2011 for Lincoln Center Out of Doors information.*)

Free concerts are also performed on Friday and Saturday evenings in the sculpture garden at the **Museum of Modern Art** (*11 W 53rd St. Tel: (212) 708 9850*).

Saturday evening performances take place on Pier 16 at **South St Seaport** (*tel: (212) 669 9400*), and across the East River a series of Celebrate Brooklyn concerts is held in **Prospect Park** (*tel: (718) 788 0055*). Central Park also hosts a festival of music – June to August – at Rumsey Field (*www.summerstage.org*).

Blue Note

Expensive but highly acclaimed, this Greenwich Village institution hosts good jazz from top performers. Cover charge varies according to star quality. There is a bar charge.
131 W 3rd St. Tel: (212) 475 8592;
www.bluenote.net

Bradley's

Greenwich Village bar where local jazz musicians gather to hear, and sometimes play with, big names. No cover charge on Mondays and Tuesdays.
70 University Place.
Tel: (212) 228 6440.

The Garage

Featuring live jazz seven nights a week, the restaurant here offers an extensive

menu of American food. Jazz lunches and brunches are also available.
99 7th Ave S. Tel: (212) 645 0600; www.garagerest.com

Iridium Jazz Club

Jazz greats and newcomers play here twice a night – at 8pm and 10pm – seven nights a week. Reserve a table online.
1650 Broadway/51st St.
Tel: (212) 582 2121;
www.iridiumjazzclub.com

Village Vanguard

The city's oldest jazz venue and still presenting big names.
178 7th Ave. Tel: (212) 255 4037;
www.villagevanguard.com

Nightclubs and discos

Bitter End

Billing itself as 'New York City's oldest rock club', the Bitter End has been presenting rock bands and singer-songwriters to its patrons since 1961.
147 Bleecker St. Tel: (212) 673 7030;
www.bitterend.com

Catch a Rising Star

A showcase club for over 20 years; famous for comedy and music by TV celebrities. New talent also gets a chance.
318 W 53rd St/8th Ave. Tel: (609) 987 8018; www.catcharisingstar.com

Kenny's Castaways

Bruce Springsteen played his first New York City show right here. There's live music here most nights of the week. Check their online calendar.
157 Bleecker St. Tel: (917) 475 1323;
www.kennyscastaways.net

Rock

Beacon Theater

Historic home of leading rock and pop acts.
2124 Broadway. Tel: (212) 465 6500;
www.beacontheatrenyc.com

Hard Rock Café

Deafening music with rock memorabilia and burgers.
1501 Broadway. Tel: (212) 343 3355;
www.hardrock.com

Madison Square Garden

Mega-rock performers play here.
7th Ave/32nd St.
Tel: (212) 465 6000;
www.thegarden.com

Catch a show on Broadway

Pyramid Club
Rock 'n' roll until 4am in this live entertainment club.
101 Ave A (6th/7th sts).
Tel: (212) 228 4888;
www.thepyramidclub.com

Radio City Music Hall
Venue for big-occasion mainstream acts.
1260 6th Ave. Tel: (212) 307 7171;
www.radiocity.com

Rodeo Bar
Loud music with Tex-Mex food. Modestly priced.
375 3rd Ave/27th St.
Tel: (212) 683 6500;
www.rodeobar.com

Film and theatre

New Yorkers are enthusiastic film- and theatre-goers. Broadway is best for the big shows and musicals, and Off-Broadway for the classics and experimental productions. Theatre, by anybody's standards, is expensive – less so in Off-Broadway playhouses – but discount tickets can be obtained (*see p179*). The *New York Times* and *Village Voice* list what's on.

La Mama Experimental Theater Company
Two theatres and a club with a wide range of avant-garde productions.
74A E 4th St. Tel: (212) 475 7710;
www.lamama.org

Pan Asian Repertory Theatre
Asian and Asian-American performers appear in new or adapted works.

ASTORIA RE-RUN

New York was a pioneer in film production when Hollywood was no more than a tract of scrubland on the outskirts of Los Angeles. The industry was firmly established in Astoria, Queens, where Paramount and other major companies were located, with stars like Gloria Swanson and Rudolph Valentino under contract.

In the early 1930s, studios began to be set up in California where the climate was more reliable for outdoor filming, and land prices were cheaper.

Astoria is now enjoying a comeback. The new studios, fourth largest in the USA, have produced *The Pink Panther* and the *Law and Order* TV series.

520 8th Ave. Tel: (212) 868 4030;
www.panasianrep.org

Playwrights Horizons
A venue for new works.
416 W 42nd St. Tel: (212) 564 1235;
www.playwrightshorizons.org

Public Theater
New and classic plays performed in this complex of five playhouses.
425 Lafayette St/Astor Pl.
Tel: (212) 539 8500;
www.publictheater.org

Generally, cinema tickets are reasonably priced, and the latest films are released first in New York. The New York Film Festival of international productions takes place in the Lincoln Center's Alice Tully Hall annually at the end of September.

Anthology Film Archives
Specialises in re-runs of film classics.
32 2nd Ave. Tel: (212) 505 5181;
www.anthologyfilmarchives.org

The **Museum of Modern Art** (*see pp70–71*) has a film library and two theatres which show classic productions, and the **Museum of the Moving Image** (*see p118*) shows foreign and avant-garde films.

Most of the big cinemas for which New York was once famous have now been converted into multi-screen complexes, with up to six films showing simultaneously. However, two houses can cope with the giant screen productions: the **Ziegfeld** (*141 W 54th St. Tel: (212) 777 3456; www.clearviewcinemas.com*) and **Radio City Music Hall** (*1260 6th Ave. Tel: (212) 247 4777*), which has a 10m (34ft)-high screen.

Christmas lights in front of Radio City Music Hall

Children

Much of the sightseeing in New York City appeals to children as much as to adults. Everyone enjoys a post-concert tour backstage at Radio City Music Hall, or finding out how the sound effects are made at the NBC.

For youngsters, there are plenty of attractions of special appeal which will also fascinate accompanying grown-ups. The **Children's Museum of Manhattan** (*see p83*) is full of high-tech

Coney Island's fairground

wonders. The accent is on self-discovery. There are enough hands-on experiences to keep children under 12 happily occupied for hours – among them, painting and other handicrafts, and trying on fancy costumes. Brooklyn also has a children's museum (*see pp108–9*).

Coney Island, one of the world's most famous seaside resorts – though heavily populated in stifling summer weather – has an amusement park (open weekends only) with roller coaster rides and games, a boardwalk, an extensive beach and a popular line in hot dogs from Nathan's. It is worth visiting even in winter, as the **New York Aquarium**, with its thousands of exotic fish, is open all year (*see pp114–15*).

The Children's Zoo in **Central Park**, where the residents are mainly pets and farm animals, also has exciting places to scramble over and through, such as a rabbit hole and Noah's Ark. The newly renovated **Central Park Zoo** includes an undercover tropical rainforest, with monkeys, reptiles and birds, and a Polar Circle, with polar bears and penguins (*see p83*).

Some sort of free entertainment – clowning or conjuring – often goes on in the park, and there is an area where the 'Frisbee rules OK'. On Saturday mornings, model boats are raced on the Conservatory Water, and on summer weekends, storytelling sessions are held by the statue of Hans Christian Andersen. Adventure playgrounds, roller skating and skateboarding, an old-fashioned carousel, puppet shows and rowing boats are among pastimes in the park.

The **Bronx Zoo** has one of the largest animal collections in North America, with a Skyfari cable car and a Bengali Express monorail providing a great view of some habitats (*see pp101–2*). Back in Manhattan, at the **World Financial Center**, make sure the children experience the two-part 'listening sculpture' in the Courtyard, where a whisper in one section is clearly heard across the room in another (*see p60*).

Go to **South Street Seaport**, too, on the East River, with its historic ships open to the public, street performers, and Seaport Experience multimedia show (*see pp48–9*).

The **Staten Island Ferry** (*see p126*) is now free for the round trip, and there are three-hour sightseeing cruises around Manhattan Island run by Circle Line at various prices.

T-rex at the American Museum of Natural History

Few children can resist a good toy shop. **FAO Schwarz** on Fifth Avenue/ 58th Street will bowl them over. The staff, in fancy costumes, provide a big welcome, and the stock is awesome and fascinating. The **Toys 'R' Us** store in Times Square has a full-size indoor Ferris wheel as well as the usual generous supply of children's goods.

Insects and reptiles, dinosaur bones and a giant stuffed whale are on show at the **American Museum of Natural History** (*see pp79–80*), and the next best thing to a personal visit to the moon can be arranged at the neighbouring **Hayden Planetarium**. These attractions, with an all-enveloping Naturemax screen, are located on Central Park West on 79th and 81st streets.

Sport and leisure

Spectator sports are to New York what gladiatorial contests were to ancient Rome – a comparison which is strengthened by the fact that Madison Square Garden (MSG), focal point of the city's sporting scene, is popularly known as the Coliseum.

Not everyone admires MSG as a building, sprawled as it is on top of Penn Station between 31st and 33rd streets at Seventh Avenue. But excitement runs high inside when a major sports event is staged there.

Hailed as the world's most famous sports, entertainment and convention complex, MSG seats more than 20,000 spectators. Ice hockey and basketball matches take place from October to April. Major international boxing matches are staged throughout the year, as well as many wrestling contests, cleverly choreographed, which get the shriekers and yellers going.

Book tickets in person at the box office, Ticketmaster (*www.ticketmaster.com*), or *www.thegarden.com*

Spectator sports
American football

New York has two teams, the Jets and the Giants, both of which play at Meadowlands. The season starts in August. Credit-card bookings can be made through Ticketmaster.

If you are in New York on the third Sunday in January, you will get caught up – like everyone else in the USA – in the excitement of the Superbowl, when the two national finalists meet. Television screening starts long before the match, and when the game starts, you may well find you get more ads than action. If you are not turned on by American football, avoid bars with big screens, where it monopolises everything. On the other hand, if you are a fan, and you cannot get to the match itself, then you know where to go!

Baseball

Played from April to October, the game lasts up to three hours and has a tremendous following. The New York Yankees play at the **Yankee Stadium** (*161st St/River Ave in the Bronx. Tel: (718) 293 4300; www.yankees.com*), and the New York Mets at **Citi Field** (*Queens. Tel: (718) 507 8499;*

www.mets.com). The champion teams of the National League and the American League meet for the final in October.

Basketball

The season starts in October, and continues until the championship matches take place in April. The game lasts only an hour, but it is 60 minutes of fast-paced action. New York has two professional teams, the Knicks (short for Knickerbockers), whose home base is Madison Square Garden, and the Mets, who play at Meadowlands.

Horse racing

Racing enthusiasts have the choice of thoroughbred and harness racing. Both types take place at Meadowlands. Trotting races are between January and August, and flat racing is from September to December.

Harness racing is in the evenings throughout the year at **Yonkers Raceway** (*tel: (914) 968 4200;*

www.yonkersraceway.com*), just north of the New York City boundary in Yonkers, Westchester County.

The **Aqueduct Racetrack** in Ozone Park, Queens, is the largest track for thoroughbred racing in the USA. Also in Queens is the **Belmont Park Racetrack**, where the Belmont Stakes, a major race in the American calendar, is run. (*For both, tel: (718) 641 4700; www.nyra.com.*)

All on-course betting is by totalisator. Off-course bets can be placed at one of a number of private OTB (Off-Track Betting) offices. Some are quite grand, with cocktail bars, restaurants and a small admission charge – and a requirement for men to wear jackets. One is the **Inside Track** (*991 2nd Ave at 52nd/53rd sts. Tel: (212) 752 1940*).

New York City Off-Track Betting (*tel: (212) 221 5200; www.nycotb.com*) is America's first government-run off-track betting operation. It has more than 100 branch offices throughout the five boroughs.

The Rangers take on the Islanders at Madison Square Garden

Ice hockey

The New York Rangers' home rink is at Madison Square Garden. The New Jersey Devils play at the Prudential Center across the Hudson River in downtown Newark, New Jersey; and the Islanders at Nassau Coliseum, Uniondale, Long Island.

Tennis

Tickets for the semi-finals and finals of the Open – the US Open Tennis Championships at the **National Tennis Centre** at Flushing Meadows, Queens – do not come cheaply, and those who wish to watch a match need to book well in advance (*tel: (718) 760 6363; www.usopen.org*).

Grandstand bleacher seating – outdoor uncovered planks (bring an inflatable cushion if your personal upholstery is inadequate) – is on a first-come first-served basis.

The Open takes place in September. In November, the annual Virginia Slims international tournament is held at Madison Square Garden.

Participatory sports

Fitness is almost a fetish with many New Yorkers, and for all its temptations – fast-food joints, hamburger and hot dog stands, happy hours and Sunday brunches – the city is a surprisingly active place.

Bicycling

The Hudson River Park Trust has completed a dedicated bicycle route that runs the length of Manhattan's West Side. *Tel: (212) 627 2020; www.hudsonriverpark.org*

Fitness

Sports Center at Chelsea Piers (*23rd St at Hudson River, West Side Highway. Tel: (212) 336 6000; www.chelseapiers.com*) has a rock-climbing wall, a 0.4km (^{1}/4-mile) indoor jogging trail, outdoor golf driving range, ice rink and general fitness centre. The **Manhattan Plaza Health Club** (*Times Square West. Tel: (212) 563 7001; www.mphc.com*) is one of the best equipped in the area, with pool, spa, tennis, climbing gym and other options.

Vanderbilt YMCA (*224 E 47th St. Tel: (212) 912 2500; www.ymcanyc.org*) has a running track, swimming pool, gymnasium and exercise classes.

Golf

Manhattan is short on space for golf courses, but outside the city limits, on Long Island, there are some of the best courses in the USA, five of them at Bethpage State Park.

Randall's Island Golf Center (*1 Randalls Island. Tel: (212) 427 5689; www.randallsislandgolfcenter.com*) offers a short game area, grass tees, battling cages and miniature golf.

Horse riding

With the closing of Claremont Riding Academy in 2007, Manhattan no longer has any riding stables. In Brooklyn, Western-style saddles are used at

Jamaica Bay Riding Academy
(*tel: (718) 531 8949; www.horsebackride. com*) for trail riding in Brooklyn's rural haunts near JFK Airport.

Ice-skating

During the winter months there is ice-skating in Central Park, at Wollman Rink at 64th Street (*tel: (212) 439 6900; www.wollmanskatingrink.com*). The sport is also catered for at several public rinks, where skates can be hired. The **Sky Rink** is one (*Chelsea Piers, Pier 61, 23rd St/Hudson River. Tel: (212) 336 6100*). It is open all year.

Small but smart, more expensive and very popular, is the one in the **Rockefeller Center** (*tel: (212) 757 5730*). It opens from 9am to midnight on Fridays and Saturdays, and until 10pm on other nights.

Jogging

Sporty types keen on keeping fit with plenty of exercise always make for **Central Park**, where jogging is the obvious (and cheapest) option. Two of the most popular trails in Manhattan are the park's Reservoir Circuit and the East River Promenade.

Joggers flock to the city in their thousands each October to take part in the New York Marathon, a 42km (26-mile) course that starts in Staten Island, then sends them streaming across the Verrazano-Narrows Bridge (out of step, hopefully), and through each of the outer boroughs before slumping across the finishing line at the Tavern on the Green in Central Park. *Entry forms: Road Runners Club, PO Box 881, FDR Station, New York, NY 10150. Tel: (212) 860 4455. For info: www.ingnycmarathon.org*

Sea fishing

Boats can be chartered for day or night sea fishing at Sheepshead Bay in South Brooklyn. The **Dorothy B VIII** (*tel: (732) 616 8378; www.dorothyb.com*) takes groups.

Swimming

New York has several pool and gymnasium complexes. Four locations are: Clarkson Street/7th Avenue (*tel: (212) 242 5228*); 342 E 54th Street (*tel: (212) 397 3154*); 59th Street/West End Avenue (*tel: (212) 397 3159*); and 35 W 134th Street (*tel: (212) 234 9603*).

Tennis

Dozens of courts are maintained by the New York City Parks Department, but the most scenic location is in **Central Park**, where there are 24 courts (*near 94th St. Tel: (212) 397 3190*). Daily and summer passes are available. Ambitious players can play where the greats gather – at the USTA **National Tennis Center** at Flushing Meadows, Queens, venue of the US Open, which has a number of outdoor and indoor courts available to the public. Those who wish to play must reserve at least two days ahead (*tel: (718) 592 8000*).

Sporting life

New Yorkers love sports – especially the kinds that exercise the throat and vocal cords, jaw muscles and drinking elbows. Among men, at least, the major American ball games, plus boxing and hockey (ice hockey, that is, of course), will break down barriers faster than a fireman's axe – and sport is the one subject almost certain to turn the most morose of

The Yankees are one of New York's most famous sports teams

Madison Square Garden, home of the New York Knicks basketball team

yellow cab drivers into a positive chatterbox.

For most events, essential requirements (for the spectator) are beer (Coke for the juniors), peanuts and popcorn, which, like hot dogs, can be bought from vendors on the terraces. It all gets noisy, agitated and rather messy as the game progresses, but there is no danger of being the victim of hooligan behaviour. American sports-watching is usually a harmless, if rowdy, pursuit.

Football has the added razzmatazz of marching bands and hyperactive cheerleaders. Baseball-viewing is slightly more sober, possibly because you need to keep your wits about you, as with cricket, to follow what is going on. Tennis is popular among both men and women here, and it's virtually impossible to get a great ticket to the US Open without some pre-planning.

Horse racing – at Aqueduct Racetrack, Queens and Belmont Park, Long Island – is as exciting as it is anywhere else in the world, but there is none of the upper-crust picnic ambience associated with European race meetings. Facilities for spectators, however, are excellent, with superb restaurants overlooking the course.

For soccer fans, you'll find many sports bars with big-screen TVs broadcasting games from around the world.

Food and drink

New York claims to offer the most diverse dining scene in the world. With so many immigrant races having settled in the city over the years, it is not surprising that the cuisine ranges from Afghan to Vietnamese. Eating out has become almost an art form.

For New Yorkers, eating out is a way of life. It is said you could try a different restaurant every night for ten years and not exhaust the possibilities. Inevitably, some close, but new ones open. More than 120 restaurants participate in the annual Summer Restaurant Week during which three-course lunch menus are offered at a fraction of their usual cost.

Price guide for dinner for one person, excluding drink and a tip:

★   inexpensive (under $30)
★★   moderate ($30–$50)
★★★   expensive ($50–$75)
★★★★ very expensive (over $75)

Main specialities to look for on the menu are suggested in some instances, though anyone intent on sampling pickled deer antler and snake wine will have to comb Chinatown or the appropriate location for themselves.

It is worth noting that most Indian restaurants are in the ★ or ★★ category and many serve lunchtime all-you-can-eat buffet meals for around $15.

Some of the more formal restaurants, especially in hotels, demand that men wear jackets and ties. Reservations are not taken by some establishments.

Check the menu to see if a service charge is imposed.

Although lots of New Yorkers love a hefty meat-based diet, vegetarians have nothing to worry about as another big chunk of the city's diners are very health-conscious. Many restaurants do cater for a wide variety of diets, including vegetarian.

Websites

New York Magazine has an excellent online database of New York restaurants, allowing you to search for anything from Afghani to Vietnamese cuisine.
http://nymag.com

Lower Manhattan

ABC Chinese Restaurant ★
Inexpensive, authentic Chinese cuisine.
34 Pell St/Mott St. Tel: (212) 346 9390.

Elephant and Castle ★

Reliable for a good square meal – burgers, omelettes, salads. No reservations. Long queues form at weekends.

68 Greenwich Ave, at the intersection of 7th Ave/11th St. Tel: (212) 243 1400; www.elephantandcastle.com

Kelley & Ping ★

By day a lively Asian grocery-cum-noodle bar, by night a slightly more sophisticated restaurant service, this noisy place is a SoHo institution where you'll get a real feel for local life.

127 Greene St, near Prince St. Tel: (212) 228 1212; www.kelleyandping.com

Adrienne's Pizza Bar ★★

Award-winning maker of square Sicilian-style pizzas draws in the financial district crowd. Brunch is served Saturday and Sunday from 11.30am to 4pm.

54 Stone St. Tel: (212) 248 3838; www.adriennespizzabar.com

Angelo of Mulberry Street ★★

Children are welcome in this typical Italian restaurant with a homely

A table with a view in Central Park

THE GREAT AMERICAN BREAKFAST

Oh, the great American breakfast! In New York you can pop into a diner for a sustaining pile of pancakes with maple syrup for a few dollars. Or you can go to a classy restaurant for the works.

How is this, for instance? Granola with berries or smoked salmon with cream cheese and bagels. Eggs Benedict or corned beef hash with egg, or smoked salmon omelette, or prime breakfast sirloin with eggs. You will almost certainly get a basket of breads, Danish pastries, fruit preserves and honey included in the cost.

Then there is coffee. Endless refills of good coffee is the American way of life!

---

atmosphere and traditional southern Italian food.

146 Mulberry St (Hester/Grand sts). Tel: (212) 966 1277; www.angelomulberry.com

Bridge Café ★★

With its waterfront building dating back to 1794, Bridge Café dubs itself 'The Oldest Drinking Establishment in New York'. City Hall politicos on both sides like this café for its seafood and informality.

279 Water St/Dover St. Tel: (212) 227 3344. www.bridgecafenyc.com

The Cupping Room ★★

Renowned for breakfast and brunch. Live music Wednesday–Saturday.

359 W Broadway/Broome St. Tel: (212) 925 2898; www.cuppingroomcafe.com

Félix ★★

French bistro style and always packed to the rafters with SoHo shoppers and

HOME COOKING

Visitors in a suite hotel with a kitchen may like to cook a meal now and again. Vegetables and fruit can be bought at green markets (some open 24 hours a day) or at farmers' markets. **Garden of Eden Gourmet Market** (*7 East 14th St, 162 W 23rd St, 2780 Broadway; www.edengourmet.com*) is a well-stocked branch of a gourmet food chain. **Dean & DeLuca** (*1150 Madison Ave at 85th St* and *560 Broadway at Prince St; www.deandeluca.com*) is another purveyor of fine food.

For a gourmet food experience, shop at the always-crowded Zabar's (*2245 Broadway, between 80th and 81st sts; www.zabars.com*), open 365 days a year. It has a kitchenware department as irresistible as the food – fresh caviar, smoked food, cheeses and take-out deli.

The Amish community sell their produce in various farmers' market locations year-round including the flagship Greenmarket at Union Square – lots of pies and pickles, and exquisitely flavoured butters and cheeses (*open: Mon, Wed, Fri & Sat*).

workers wolfing down classic dishes like *moules frites* and *steak au poivre*.
340 W Broadway/Grand St. Tel: (212) 431 0021; www.felixnyc.com/soho/

Fig & Olive ★★
Fresh, inventive food – pasta, meat and poultry – served in a light and airy dining room.
420 W 13th St/9th Ave. Tel: (212) 924 1200; www.figandolive.com

Il Cortile ★★
Very popular restaurant specialising in northern Italian cuisine, with an attractive conservatory-style dining room. Noteworthy veal and pasta dishes.
125 Mulberry St/Hester St. Tel: (212) 226 6060; www.ilcortile.com

L'Ecole ★★
The restaurant at the French Culinary Institute offers eclectic French favourites cooked and served by students. Four- and five-course prix fixe available at dinnertime.
462 Broadway/Grand St. Tel: (212) 324 2433; www.frenchculinary.com

Les Halles Downtown ★★
An excellent Parisian-style brasserie from famed celebrity chef Anthony Bourdain. Specialities include *coq au vin*, blood sausages with caramelised apples, and *côte de boeuf*.
12 John St at Broadway. Tel: (212) 285 8585. www.leshalles.net

Peking Duck House ★★
Peking duck in a plain setting; satisfying duck soups.
28 Mott St/Canal Square. Tel: (212) 227 1810; www. pekingduckhousenyc.com Also at 236 E 53rd St (2nd/3rd aves). Tel: (212) 759-8260.

Shang ★★
A different sort of Chinatown experience, this dining spot is located on the second floor of Thompson Les hotel.
187 Orchard St/E Houston. Tel: (212) 260 7900; www.shangrestaurant.com

Tribeca Grill ★★
Robert De Niro's place, with his father's paintings brightening up the walls and people from the film studios above hanging out. The food is sophisticated and the wine list runs to 1,900 bottles.
375 Greenwich St/ Franklin St. Tel:

(212) 941 3900; www. myriadrestaurantgroup.com

Aquagrill ★★★

Fresh fare to fill plates and appetites.

210 Spring St/ Ave of the Americas. Tel: (212) 274 0505.

Balthazar Restaurant ★★★

Begin your meal with the excellent onion soup *gratinee* and continue with items from the raw bar. For your main meal you won't know which to choose: duck shepherd's pie, *steak frites* or Berkshire pork porterhouse.

80 Spring St (Broadway/Crosby sts).

Tel: (212) 965 1414; www.balthazarny.com

Chez Jacqueline ★★★

The owner, from Nice, concentrates on Mediterranean flavours, including French-style tapas and Italian risotto, in a romantic setting helped by the rustic brick bar.

72 MacDougal St (Houston/Bleecker sts). Tel: (212) 505 0727; www. chezjacquelinerestaurant. com

Chinatown Brasserie ★★★

Renowned for excellent dim sum, and a lively bar, this huge place is amazingly popular.

380 Lafayette St, at

Great Jones St. Tel: (212) 533 7000; www. chinatownbrasserie.com

Five Points ★★★

Locals rave about the 'out-of-this-world' food here, where chef Marc Meyer produces hearty and flavourful American-Mediterranean fusion food.

31 Great Jones St (Lafayette/Bowery). Tel: (212) 253 5700; www. fivepointsrestaurant.com

Landmarc ★★★

If you fancy steak but your partner wants French or Italian, then head for Marc Murphy's, which caters to all those

(Cont. on p162)

The Balthazar Restaurant on Spring Street

Fast food

Ask for a Coney Islander in a snack bar and you will probably get a puzzled stare. Invented about 100 years ago, it has long since changed its name to the hot dog, and out of hundreds of hot dog stands, probably the most famous is on Brooklyn's Coney Island, where it was invented. New York City offers a good variety of fast food. The ubiquitous hamburger has travelled a long way since its origins in the small town of Hamburg in upstate New York, near Niagara Falls. Its predecessor was the pork pattie, but the two brothers who had a food concession at the 1885

Fast-food advertising

Hamburg Fair ran out of pork, and improvised with minced beef, adding

Fast food fits the pace and style of this busy city

An American diner, as seen in a hundred films

such unlikely things as brown sugar and coffee to get a satisfactory taste. Garnished with onions, catsup (ketchup) and mustard, it has been flavour of the decades ever since.

Jewish fast foods that most people enjoy are bagels and blintzes. Bagels are rings of hard bread, often toasted. Blintzes are crêpes filled with fruit or cheese and served with sour cream.

There is always a bite to eat on street corners. Pretzels and roasted peanuts are popular. Many bars and diners offer free snacks with drinks during the weekday happy hour – usually a couple of hours. Or try one of the low-cost 24-hour eateries like Manhattan's Empire Diner at 210 Tenth Avenue and 22nd Street (*www.empire-diner.com*), where live piano music accompanies the simple American fare. Pastarias are all over town, and coffee shops are often good for home-cooked snacks.

Quick snacks are available for busy people on the move

tastes on the excellent eclectic menu.

179 W Broadway (Leonard/Worth sts). Tel: (212) 343 3883 (also at 10 Columbus Cr, 3rd fl at the Time Warner Center, Tel: (212) 823 6123); www.landmarc-restaurant.com

Mercer Kitchen ★★★

Always packed, this Jean-George establishment serves everything from cheeseburgers to roasted lobster to duck confit at dinner.

99 Prince St/Mercer St. Tel: (212) 966 5454; www.jean-georges.com

Minetta Tavern ★★★

Italian cuisine from noon to midnight.

113 MacDougal St/Minetta Lane. Tel: (212) 475 3850; www. minettatavernny.com

Spice Market ★★★

Inspired by the traditional street foods of Asia, this Jean-George Vongerichten-run restaurant offers full dinner and tasting menus.

403 W 13th St/9th Ave. Tel: (212) 675 2322; www.spicemarketnewyork. com

Bouley ★★★★

Considered by many to be the best restaurant in New York. World-class French cuisine.

163 Duane St/Hudson. Tel: (212) 964 2525; www.davidbouley.com

Buddakan ★★★★

A chic see-and-be-seen hotspot serving modern Asian cuisine.

75 9th Ave/16th St. Tel: (212) 989 6699; www.buddakannyc.com

Gotham Bar & Grill ★★★★

Inventive New American cooking.

12 E 12th St (5th Ave/University Pl). Tel: (212) 620 4020; www. gothambarandgrill.com

Nobu ★★★★

Gastronomic treasures from chef Nobuyuki Matuhisa's kitchen. Japanese cuisine as you've never tasted it before.

105 Hudson St/Franklin St. Tel: (212) 219 0500; www. noburestaurants.com

One If By Land, Two If By Sea ★★★★

Beef Wellington by candelight in this 1786 stone carriage house.

17 Barrow St. Tel: (212) 255 8649; www.oneifbyland.com

Wallse ★★★★

Big flavours of Viennese cuisine, enough to make diners waltz.

344 W 11th St. Tel: (212) 352 2300; www. wallserestaurant.com

Midtown Manhattan

Hakata Grill ★

Round off a theatre trip with noodles and affordable sushi.

231 E 53rd St (2nd/3rd aves). Tel: (212) 245 1020; www.hakatagrill.com

Old Town Bar ★

The food here is standard pub grub, but this traditional Victorian tavern is friendly, if noisy.

45 E 18th St (Broadway/ Park Ave South). Tel: (212) 529 6732; www.oldtownbar.com

Planet Hollywood ★

The bicycle from Butch Cassidy and the Sundance Kid and masses more film memorabilia are part of the décor at this high-vitality experience. Wide choice of good, quick

food, plenty of it, and rich desserts.
1540 Broadway/45th St. Tel: (212) 337 7827; www. planethollywood.com

Woo Chon ★
A range of authentic hearty dishes at great value at this convivial Korean restaurant with a waterfall feature. Delicious seafood pancakes are among the foods on the menu.
8–10 W 36th St (5th/6th aves). Tel: (212) 695 0676; www.woochonny.com

Chez Napoléon ★★
Frogs' legs Provençale, bouillabaisse and rabbit in wine are specialities.
365 W 50th St (8th/9th aves). Tel: (212) 265 6980; www.cheznapoleon.com

Dawat ★★
Service is excellent at this well-liked Indian restaurant. Offerings at the lunch buffet are extensive.
210 E 58th St/2nd Ave. Tel: (212) 355-7555; dawatrestaurant.com

Markt ★★
Range of mussels and other Belgian fare, and good beer.
676 Sixth Ave/21st St. Tel: (212) 727 3314; www. marktrestaurant.com

Oyster Bar & Restaurant ★★
One of New York's great experiences. Opened in 1913. Huge variety of delectable fresh fish, oyster stew, pan roasts and desserts. Counter and table service.
Grand Central Station

Lower Level, between Vanderbilt/Lexington aves. Tel: (212) 490 6650; www.oysterbarny.com

Russian Samovar ★★
No-frills décor, but good food brings clients back again and again to this Theater District restaurant. Live Russian music with dinner.
256 W 52nd St (Broadway/8th Ave). Tel: (212) 757 0168; www.russiansamovar.com

Shun Lee Palace ★★
Beautifully prepared cuisine from the regions of Hunan, Beijing, Shanghai and Canton.
155 E 55th St/3rd Ave. Tel: (212) 371 8844; shunleepalace.com

Victor's Café 52 ★★
A Cuban classic in tropical setting. Stone crabs, paella, roast suckling pig and black bean soup in skylit rooms. Tapas bar. Soft piano music and a strolling violinist.
236 W 52nd St (Broadway/8th Ave). Tel: (212) 586 7714; www.victorscafe.com

Zen Palate ★★
A delight for vegetarians and the generally health-

Catch of the day in Chinatown

conscious – tofu comes in many forms.
34 Union Sq E/16th St.
Tel: (212) 614 9345;
www.zenpalate.com

Barbetta ★★★
Excellent Italian cuisine is served in antique-filled elegantly formal surroundings in the heart of the Theater District. In summer you can relax in the garden.
321 W 46th St
(8th/9th aves).
Tel: (212) 246 9171; www.
barbettarestaurant.com

Giorgio's of Gramercy ★★★
This sophisticated but friendly place has gained a great local reputation for its quality Italian-American nouveau cuisine combined with reasonable prices.
27 E 21st St (Park Ave
South/Broadway).
Tel: (212) 477 0007; www.
giorgiosofgramercy.com

Mesa Grill ★★★
Now an established house for southwestern grills.
102 5th Ave (15th/16th
sts). Tel: (212) 807 7400;
www.mesagrill.com/
newyorkcity

The Oak Room ★★★
This clubby room at The Plaza Hotel has a long history, starting as a men's-only bar in 1907.
10 Central Park South.
Tel: (212) 758 7777;
www.oakroomny.com

Periyali ★★★
Better-than-average upscale Greek restaurant, presenting herby grills – including octopus – and pleasantly informal.
35 W 20th St
(5th/6th aves).
Tel: (212) 463 7890;
www.periyali.com

Sardi's ★★★
This Broadway legend continues to pull in the tourists and local inhabitants.
234 W 44th St
(7th/8th aves).
Tel: (212) 221 8440;
www.sardis.com

Union Square Café ★★★
Media people in the area flock to this ever-popular American restaurant.
21 E 16th St (Union
Square/5th Ave).
Tel: (212) 243 4020; www.
unionsquarecafe.com

Aquavit ★★★★
Scandinavian specialities – venison with juniper sauce, gravlax with mustard sauce – in former Rockefeller town house with a six-storey atrium with waterfall.
65 E 55th St
(Park/Madison aves).
Tel: (212) 307 7311;
www.aquavit.org

Le Bernardin ★★★★
One of the classiest French restaurants in the city, this is fine dining New York style with the focus on fish, from almost raw oysters to pan roasted monkfish to baked lobster on a bed of truffled foie gras stuffing.
155 W 51st St
(6th/7th aves).
Tel: (212) 554 1515;
www.le-bernardin.com

Remi ★★★★
High-class Italian restaurant, where people go to see and be seen, and to enjoy the risotto and pasta.
145 W 53rd St
(6th/7th aves).
Tel: (212) 581 4242;
www.remi-ny.com

The View ★★★★
No tourist should miss New York's only revolving restaurant, located high above Times Square. International cuisine. Pre-theatre menu is available. Amazing view.

Marriott Marquis Hotel,
1535 Broadway
(45th/46th sts).
Tel: (212) 704 8900.

Upper Manhattan

Amor Cubano ★
Tasty ethnic food
with live music
Wednesday to Sunday,
7–11pm.
2018 Third Ave/111th St.
Tel: (212) 996 1220; www.
amorcubanorestaurant.
com

Big Daddy's ★
A kitschy diner offering
standard burgers, tater
tots and milkshakes.
1596 2nd Ave/83rd St.
Tel: (212) 717 2020;
www.bigdaddysnyc.com

Chez Lucienne ★
Classic French with
a twist – every
Wednesday is 'Couscous
Night' complete with
a belly dancing show
at 8.30pm.
308 Lenox Ave.
Tel: (212) 289 5555;
www.chezlucienne.com

Cleopatra's Needle ★
Jazz, jam sessions and
good Middle Eastern food.
2485 Broadway
(92nd/93rd sts).
Tel: (212) 769 6969; www.
cleopatrasneedleny.com

Ellen's Stardust ★
Back to the 1950s with
shake, rattle and roll and
vintage music, Pink Lady
cocktails and grilled
swordfish steaks.
1650 Broadway/51st St.
Tel: (212) 956 5151; www.
ellensstardustdiner.com

Havana Central ★
Indulge in the flavours of
Cuba with lobster stuffed
avocado, home-made
tamales and sugar-cane
lime chicken salad.
2911 Broadway/113thSt.
Tel: (212) 662 8830;
www.havanacentral.com

**Sylvia's Soul Food
Restaurant ★**
Southern staples like spicy
barbecued ribs, fried
chicken, pecan pie and
greens to set you alight.
328 Lenox Ave
(126th/127th sts).
Tel: (212) 996 0660;
www.sylviassoulfood.com

Afghan Kebab House ★★
High-value, low-cost
kebabs and other savoury
ethnic food. Bring your
own alcoholic beverage.
1345 2nd Ave
(70th/71st sts).
Tel: (212) 517 2776.

Café Greco ★★
Mediterranean dishes
from France, Italy, North
Africa and Greece. Also
high-value fixed-price
option – all in an
attractive, split-level
atrium setting.
1390 2nd Ave (71st/
72nd sts).
Tel: (212) 737 4300.

Cotton Club ★★
The Harlem legend keeps
moving but keeps open,
serving soul food from
(Cont. on p168)

A 1950s American experience awaits at Ellen's Stardust diner

Nightlife

New York is definitely the city that never sleeps and you'll find all manner of bars, nightclubs, discos and comedy clubs to keep you occupied. Whether you're looking to discover the next rock sensation or indulge in some drinks and jazz, you'll find what you're searching for in Manhattan and its boroughs.

The first thing to remember is that there is a distinction between the nightclubs Manhattan residents frequent and those that are favoured by the 'bridge and tunnel crowd' that live in the city's outer limits. New Yorkers gravitate to the edgier establishments and the bouncers there are picky about whom they let beyond the velvet rope. At 'commuter bars', you'll see many people still dressed in their work clothes – be that a suit and tie or more blue-collar fare. Both ends of the spectrum provide visitors with unlimited evening entertainment.

Irish pubs are popular all over the city. Some of the most well known include McSorley's Old Ale House at

The Dubliner Pub is popular day and night

Ablaze with colourful lights and neon signs, Times Square at night is a must-see for many tourists

15 E 7th St (*2nd/3rd aves;*
www.mcsorleysnewyork.com), The
Dubliner at 45 Stone St (*Coenties*
Aly/Mill Ln) and Pig 'n' Whistle Times
Square (*165 W 47th St/7th Ave;*
www.pignwhistlets.com). Even those
without an Irish accent are given a
warm welcome.

Christopher Street in the West
Village (*between W 4th St and*
Waverly Pl) has a vibrant gay/lesbian
scene. It's also a neighbourhood
steeped in history; the Stonewall Inn,
site of the 1969 riots and epicentre of
the gay liberation movement, was
located here.

If you spend time in Manhattan
you'll no doubt come across the seedy
underbelly of the city and that
includes the peepshows that line the
western edge of Times Square. If
you're looking for something a bit

tamer, try one of the city's billiard
establishments: Amsterdam Billiards in
Union Square (*110 E 11th St/4th Ave.*
Tel: (212) 995 0333;
www.amsterdambilliardclub.com) or
Eastside Billiards (*163 E 86th St.*
(Lexington/3rd Ave); Tel: (212) 831
POOL; www.eastsidebilliards.com).

Two good nightclub directories
are published by *New York*
Magazine (*www.nymag.com/nightlife*)
and *Time Out New York* (*www.*
newyork.timeout.com/section/clubs).

Whatever your preference, you'll
find a night-time hangout that meets
with your approval. Most bars and
clubs stay open until between 2am
and 4am (legal closing time). Be sure
to tip the bartender at least $1 per
drink or 15–20 per cent of your total
bill if you're sitting at a table served
by a waiter or waitress.

SUNDAY BRUNCH

This is an institution in New York. Some restaurants provide full waiter service. Others offer buffet-style food beautifully displayed.

Brunchtime varies slightly, but is usually somewhere between 11am and 4pm.

'Eat where the locals go' is always good advice. The Mark Hotel has a loyal following among its neighbours in E 77th Street and the Madison Avenue area. With visitors, too, it is busy every Sunday at brunchtime.

Choose from the menu – diver scallops with warm black truffle toast, Alsatian onion tart, oatmeal soufflé and veal Milanese with green beans and shallots are among the options – or go for prix fixe, with a choice of two or three courses.

the South and a hot gospel ambience for Sunday brunch.
656 W 125th St (Broadway/Riverside Dr). Tel: (212) 663 7980; www.cottonclub-newyork.com

Darbar ★★
Well above average Indian restaurant specialising in tandoori dishes, *saag gosht*, crab Malabar and lamb kebab Punjabi.
152 E 46th St/Lexington. Tel: (212) 681 4500; www.1darbarnyc.com

Isabella's ★★
Creative food with dining inside or out, especially good for Sunday brunch.
359 Columbus Ave/ 77th St. Tel: (212) 724 2100; www. brguestrestaurants.com

Joe Allen ★★
Theatrical habitat that brings out the stars and the stargazers and serves homey favourites like roasted beef marrow and macaroni and cheese.
326 W 46th St (8th/9th aves). Tel: (212) 581 6464; www. joeallenrestaurant.com

Le Relais de Venise ★★
Parisian-style bistro serving the best *steak frites* and green salad with walnuts and mustard vinaigrette.
590 Lexington Ave/ 52nd St. Tel: (212) 758 3989; www.relaisdevenise.com

Le Rivage ★★
Generous portions of traditional bistro fare that many consider to be the best French buy in the Theater District. The fixed-price dinner is a bargain.
340 W 46th St (8th/9th aves). Tel: (212) 765 7374;

www.lerivagenyc.com

Nancy's Pig Heaven ★★
Pork (as you might have guessed) is the speciality in this popular Chinese East Sider.
1540 2nd Ave (80th/81st sts). Tel: (212) 744 4887; www.pigheaven.biz

Pasha ★★
Traditional Turkish lamb, quail and aubergine-based cuisine.
170 W 71st St/Columbus Ave. Tel: (212) 579 8751; www.pashanewyork.com

Pinocchio Ristorante ★★
The locals like this restaurant on the Upper East Side where the owner waits on tables and the Italian food and atmosphere are both terrific.
1748 1st Ave (90th/91st sts). Tel: (212) 828 5810.

Russian Vodka Room ★★
A dark bar and

restaurant full of the atmosphere of the former USSR, with the compensation of a choice of over 50 vodkas.
265 W 52nd St (Broadway/8th aves). Tel: (212) 307 5835; www. russianvodkaroom.com

Sarabeth's Kitchen ★★
Informal dining in pleasant, home-like, no-smoking atmosphere. Interesting menus. Locations throughout the city.
1295 Madison Ave/92nd St. Tel: (212) 410 7335; www.sarabethseast.com

Sushi Zen ★★
Elegantly served sushi in a tranquil setting.
108 W 44th St (6th/7th aves). Tel: (212) 302 0707; www.sushizen-ny.com

Vico ★★
Noisy, and not cheap, this Italian restaurant nevertheless attracts the crowds because the food is consistently inspired. Cash only.
1302 Madison Ave/92nd St. Tel: (212) 876 2222.

Frankie & Johnnie's ★★★
Landmark restaurant famous for steaks, chops and seafood since 1926.
269 W 45th St (7th/8th aves). Tel: (212) 997 9494; www. frankieandjohnnies.com

The Mark Restaurant by Jean Georges ★★★
This is the celebrated restaurant in Manhattan, run by Jean-George Vongerichten and located within The Mark Hotel.

Mark Hotel, 25 E 77th St/Madison Ave. Tel: (212) 744 4300; www.themarkhotel.com

Mermaid Inn Uptown ★★★
A funky seafood spot offering whole roasted fish, grilled shrimp, lobster sandwiches and more.
568 Amsterdam Ave/87th St. Tel: (212) 799 7400; www.themermaidnyc.com

Ouest ★★★
Top-notch French gourmet cooking in the unlikely setting of the Upper West Side, and in an unlikely, relaxed, family-style restaurant. Chef Tom Valenti's dishes appeal to everyone who likes good food, and roasted

The Cupping Room is a favourite for brunch

The River Café – good food in superb surroundings

pork tenderloin is just one of the signature dishes that have made his name.
2315 Broadway/84th St. Tel: (212) 580 8700; www.ouestny.com

Pappardella ★★★
A neighbourhood favourite serving the freshest pasta this side of Italy.
316 Columbus Cr. Tel: (212) 595 7996; www.pappardella.com

Post House ★★★
An American steakhouse *par excellence.* Superior wine list, beef served ten different ways, and superb seafood. Try chilled baby lobster as an appetiser.
28 E 63rd St (Madison/Park aves).
Tel: (212) 935 2888; www.theposthouse.com

Rock Center Cafe ★★★
Classical American cooking served with a view of the ice rink or summer garden, depending on season.
Rockefeller Center, 20 W 50th St. Tel: (212) 332 7620; www.patinagroup.com

Daniel ★★★★
This special-occasion French restaurant embraces gracious service and is reputed to be the place where many New Yorkers 'pop the question'.
60 E 65th St. Tel: (212) 288 0033; www.danielnyc.com

Le Périgord ★★★★
Aficionados say this is one of the best classic French restaurants in town. It has offered a fine dining experience for many years. Do make a reservation.
405 E 52nd St/1st Ave. Tel: (212) 755 6244; www.leperigord.com

Petrossian ★★★★
The Petrossian family is a leading importer of caviar to the USA, and the ornate restaurant entices gourmets with pre- and post-theatre offerings of Beluga, Ostera and Sevruga caviar – now a rarity.
182 W 58th St/7th Ave. Tel: (212) 245 2214; www.petrossian.com

The Bronx

Dominick's ★★
Communal tables, no menu, and plenty of fun and southern Italian food for everyone.
2335 Arthur Ave (3rd Ave/187th St). Tel: (718) 733 2807.

Brooklyn

Tripoli ★
Cavernous place with exceptionally good Lebanese food (also to take away). Able to

Food and drink

accommodate larger
groups.
*156 Atlantic Ave/
Clinton St.
Tel: (718) 596 5800;
www.tripolirestaurant.com*
Henry's End ★★
American cooking with a
French accent on fish
and game.
*44 Henry St/Cranberry St.
Tel: (718) 834 1776;
www.henrysend.com*
Queen ★★
Upmarket Italian
restaurant with high-
class clientele.
*84 Court St (Livingstone/
Schermerhorn sts).
Tel: (718) 596 5954;
www.queenrestaurant.com*
Restaurant 101 ★★
A popular haunt with
young locals, this
cheerful eatery serves up
pizza and pasta among
other popular dishes.
10018 4th Ave/100th St.

The best of Chinese cuisine

*Tel: (718) 833 1313;
www.101nyc.com*
Peter Luger ★★★★
Big T-bone steaks at this
no-frills 1887 restaurant.
The dull décor does not
deter the crowds.
*178 Broadway/Driggs Ave.
Tel: (718) 387 7400;
www.peterluger.com*
River Café ★★★★
Highly prestigious
restaurant with one of
New York's most creative
chefs. Sample his Wagyu
steak tartare, followed by
crisp duck breast with
white truffle honey and
fennel pollen glaze.
*Under the Brooklyn
Bridge, 1 Water St,
Brooklyn Heights.
Tel: (718) 522 5200;
www.rivercafe.com*

Queens
Piccola Venezia ★★
A family-owned

restaurant, offering
authentic northern Italian
food in a bustling setting.
*42–01 28th Ave/42nd St.
Tel: (718) 721 8470;
www.piccola-venezia.com*
Water's Edge ★★★★
Contemporary American
cuisine. Formal dining
aboard a barge with a
view of the Manhattan
skyline.
*East River, 401 44th Dr,
Long Island City.
Tel: (718) 482 0033;
www.watersedgenyc.com*

Staten Island
Brioso Ristorante ★★
Family-friendly Italian
restaurant where most of
the menu is available in
child-sized portions, and
there's a good wine list to
appeal to the adults, too.
You may have to queue at
busy times, but it's worth
the wait.
*174 New Dorp Ln/9th St.
Tel: (718) 667 1700;
www.briosoristorante.com*
Nove Italian Bistro ★★
Southern Italian cuisine
in a friendly family
restaurant with a trendy
bar.
*3900 Richmond Ave.
Tel: (718) 227 3286; www.
noveitalianbistro.com*

Accommodation

There's no way to sugarcoat it: New York City lodgings – especially those uptown – are not inexpensive. Posh hotels and those centrally located are the first to book up. However, New York City's excellent transit system of subways and buses mean's that you really can stay just about anywhere and get to the action fairly quickly.

New York welcomes travellers from all walks of life. Whether you're seeking luxurious penthouse accommodation offering breathtakingly expansive views of Central Park or much cheaper hostel rooms, you'll find whatever you seek.

Begin your search for accommodation by determining which points of interest you'll most likely visit. Museum buffs often stay somewhere in Upper Manhattan. Families and those who plan to visit sites like the Empire State Building and Times Square often prefer the convenience of midtown. Lower Manhattan is dotted with trendy boutique-style hotels, affordable B&B accommodation, and some very affordable hostels.

Prices are based on the lowest published rate for a standard double room per night, not including taxes and fees:

★   inexpensive (under $100)
★★   moderate ($100–$300)
★★★   expensive ($300–$500)
★★★★   very expensive (over $500)

Websites

NYC & Company, the City's tourism organisation, maintains an extensive database of accommodation at *www.nycgo.com*

Lower Manhattan

Jazz on the Town Hostel ★

This four-storey East Village hostel offers dorm-style rooms with attached bathrooms in 4-, 6- and 8-bed configurations.
307 E 14th St (1st/2nd aves).
Tel: (212) 228 2780; www.jazzhostels.com

Andaz Wall Street ★★

Managed by Hyatt, check-in takes place in the lounge by a host with a hand-held PC. Rooms are spacious and modern.
75 Wall St (Water/Pearl sts).
Tel: (212) 590 1234;
www.newyork.wallstreet.andaz.hyatt.com

Hampton Manhattan Seaport-Financial District ★★

Clean and comfortable, the 65-room hotel offers free Internet and a hot breakfast daily.

*320 Pearl St
(Peck Slip/Dover St).
Tel: (212) 571 4400;
hamptoninn.hilton.com*

Wall Street Inn ★★

Near the New York City
Stock Exchange, the inn
features an early
American design motif.
Free buffet breakfast is
offered daily.

*9 S William St/Mill Ln.
Tel: (212) 747 1500;
www.thewallstreetinn.com*

**Washington Square
Hotel ★★**

Parents visiting their New
York University students
frequent this Greenwich
Village favourite. Book
early for stays during the
school year.

*103 Waverly Pl/
MacDougal St.
Tel: (212) 777 9515;
www.wshotel.com*

Millenium Hilton ★★★

Typical chain hotel
located in the World
Trade Center/Financial
District.

*55 Church St (Dey/Vesey
sts). Tel: (212) 693 2001;
www.newyorkmillenium.
hilton.com*

**Ritz-Carlton Battery
Park ★★★**

Rooms and suites have
fantastic views of either

the Statue of Liberty or
the skyline of Lower
Manhattan.

*Two West St
(Battery Pl/1st Pl).
Tel: (212) 344 0800;
www.ritzcarlton.com*

SoHo Grand ★★★

Fun boutique hotel
offering extras like iPods
and bicycles to use
during your stay, or a
bowl of goldfish to
brighten your room.
There are also specially
designed rooms for
families travelling
with babies or small
children.

*310 Broadway/Grand St.
Tel: (212) 965 3000;
www.sohogrand.com*

Midtown

Chelsea Hostel ★

Well-located hostel
offers both private and
dorm-style rooms.
Rates include continental
breakfast.

*251 W 20th St
(7th/8th aves).
Tel: (212) 647 0010;
www.chelseahostel.com*

Vanderbilt YMCA ★

Benefits of staying at
the 'Y' include a
multilingual staff,
access to YMCA
fitness facilities and
free Wi-Fi.

*224 East 47th St
(2nd/3rd aves).
Tel: (212) 912 2500;
www.ymcanyc.org*

The swanky Plaza Hotel near Central Park

Marriott Marquis ★★
Stay in the very heart of Times Square at this high-rise hotel complete with a revolving restaurant at the top.
1535 Broadway(45th/46th sts). Tel: (212) 398 1900; www.marriott.com

Inn at Irving Place ★★★
Staying in one of the 12 guest rooms or suites at this unmarked town house will make you feel like a true New Yorker. Décor harks back to the late 19th century.
56 Irving Pl 1(7th/18th sts). Tel: (212) 533 4600; www.innatirving.com

Inn on 23rd ★★★
A friendly urban B&B offering personal service in a renovated 19th-century town house.
131 W 23rd St (6th/7th aves). Tel: (212) 463 0330; www.innon23rd.com

Le Parker Meridien ★★★
Chic hotel close to Central Park. Don't miss Norma's, off the lobby, for the best breakfast – served all day – in Manhattan. It's also one of the few Manhattan hotels with a pool.
119 W 56th St (6th/7th aves).

The New York Palace, 455 Madison Avenue

Tel: (212) 245 5000; www.parkermeridien.com

Library Hotel ★★★
Each floor of this hotel is devoted to a category of the Dewey Decimal System, including Literature, Languages, History, Maths & Science, and Technology. Rooms are decorated with art and books related to the designated subject.
299 Madison Ave/41st St. Tel: (212) 983 4500; www.libraryhotel.com

Four Seasons ★★★★
This luxury hotel was designed by the reknowned IM Pei. It has exceptional views of Manhattan.
57 E 57th St (Park/Madison aves). Tel: (212) 758 5700; www.fourseasons.com/ newyorkfs

The Peninsula ★★★★
The Peninsula's flagship location in the United States, this de-luxe hotel is located in a 1905 Beaux-Arts landmark building.
700 5th Ave/55th St. Tel: (212) 956 2888; www. newyork.peninsula.com

St Regis ★★★★
Butler service sets this luxury hotel apart. It has 13 types of suite – including the one-of-a-kind 158sq-metre (1,700sq ft) Bottega Veneta Suite.
2 E 55th St/5th Ave. Tel: (212) 753 4500; www.stregis.com

Upper Manhattan
Candy Hostel ★
Inexpensive uptown hostel near Central Park

offering shared and private rooms – all with free Internet.

316 W 95th St (West End Ave/Riverside Dr).
Tel: (212) 866 1420;
www.candynyc.com

West Side YMCA ★

You won't find cheerier or less expensive options in the area. Single and double private rooms are available.

5 W 63rd St (Broadway/Central Park West).
Tel: (212) 875 4100;
www.ymcanyc.org

Beacon Hotel ★★

On a tree-lined street on the Upper West Side, Beacon Hotel is known for its oversized rooms and views of Central Park, the Hudson River, and Midtown.

2130 Broadway/75th St.
Tel: (212) 787 1100;
www.beaconhotel.com

The Lucerne ★★

This affordable hotel puts emphasis on service and delivers with amenities like its complimentary wine hour every Thursday night.

201 W 79th St/Amsterdam Ave.
Tel: (212) 875 1000;
www.thelucernehotel.com

The Carlyle ★★★★

This New York institution welcomes travellers, writers, artists and world leaders. Guest rooms and suites are offered alongside residential apartments.

35 E 76th St (Madison/Park aves).
Tel: (212) 744 1600;
www.thecarlyle.com

Hotel Plaza Athénée ★★★★

New suites at this East Side hotel now feature hardwood floors and marble bathrooms.

37 E 64th St (Park/Madison aves).
Tel: (212) 734 9100;
www.plaza-athenee.com

Mandarin Oriental New York ★★★★

This high-end hotel atop the Time Warner Center towers over Columbus Circle at the southwest end of Central Park. Guestroom views provide the 'wow' factor.

80 Columbus Cr/60th St.
Tel: (212) 805 8800; www.mandarinoriental.com/newyork

The Pierre ★★★★

This landmark hotel recently underwent a $100 million renovation of the lobby and public areas as well as all guest rooms and suites. Staff outnumber guests three to one.

2 E 61st St/5th Ave.
Tel: (212) 838 8000;
www.tajhotels.com

The Grand Hyatt, Park Avenue at Grand Central Station

Practical guide

Arriving

Documentation

Passports are required by all visitors to the USA. Visas are required by all except Canadians, New Zealanders and UK citizens visiting for business or tourism for a stay of not more than 90 days, provided that an onward or return ticket is held and that they are arriving in the USA on a participating carrier. UK citizens and New Zealanders must also have completed a visa waiver form, usually completed during the outward flight or on arrival at the airport. Those covered by the visa waiver programme must also have valid ESTA (Electronic System Travel Authorisation). This should be obtained no less than 72 hours before travel (*http://esta.cbp.dhs.gov*). While in the USA, visitors can take a side trip overland or by sea to Canada or Mexico and re-enter the USA without a visa within the 90-day period. This rule also applies to nationals of most other European countries and Japan. These regulations are constantly being checked and sometimes changed, in the fight against terrorism, so always double-check the current situation.

By air

New York is served by three airports: John F Kennedy (JFK) International and LaGuardia, both in Queens, and Newark International in New Jersey.

LaGuardia mainly handles domestic services. A recorded information service covering all three airports is operated by the MTA of New York and New Jersey (*tel: (800) 247 7433*).

Airport transfers

JFK Airport (*tel: (718) 244 4444; www.kennedyairport.com*) is 24km (15 miles) from mid-Manhattan. There are taxi stands outside all terminals and a flat fee is charged, plus the cost of any tolls, and a tip. Current cost to mid-Manhattan is about $45.

JFK is served by the Howard Beach subway station, which is on the A line. To get there take the AirTrain from all JFK terminals. Stops are made throughout Queens, Brooklyn, Manhattan and via transfer to other subway lines to the Bronx. Fare is $2.25 (cash or Metrocard). There is an additional $5 charge for AirTrain. Travel time is approximately 60–75 minutes from JFK to mid-Manhattan.

There are several bus options from JFK to various parts of New York. The **New York Airport Service Express Bus** (*tel: (718) 875 8200; www.nyairportservice.com*) runs a service to Grand Central Station and then on to the Port Authority and Penn Station every 15–30 minutes from 6.15am–11.10pm. The journey time is 45–60 minutes, but can be longer at peak times.

SuperShuttle Manhattan (*tel: (212) 209 7000 or (212) 258 3826 or (800) 258 3826; www.supershuttle.com*) provides a shared-ride van service 24/7 to several addresses in Manhattan, including major hotels. Advance booking is not necessary but can be done on their website or by phone. They provide the same service from LaGuardia Airport.

New York City Transit (*tel: (718) 330 1234; www.mta.info*) runs the Q3 and Q10 bus to Queens and the B15 to East New York and Brooklyn. **Trans-Bridge Lines** (*tel: (610) 868 6001; www.transbridgelines.com*) runs several buses per day to the Port Authority Bus Terminal, 42nd Street and 8th Ave.

LaGuardia Airport (*tel: (718) 533 3400; www.laguardiaairport.com*) is 13km (8 miles) from mid-Manhattan. Taxi fares will be on the meter, plus any tolls payable, and a tip. Fares range from $21–30 into Manhattan. There is no convenient subway service for LaGuardia.

Possible bus options include **SuperShuttle Manhattan** (*see below*) and the **New York Airport Service Express Bus** (*tel: (718) 875 8200; www.nyairportservice.com*), which runs a service to Grand Central Station, the Port Authority Bus Terminal and Penn Station every 20–30 minutes from 7.20am–11pm. There are several other bus services to areas including Queens, which give subway connections into Manhattan. See the airport website for current information.

Newark Liberty International Airport (*tel: (973) 961 6000; www.newarkairport.com*) is about 26km (16 miles) from midtown. At Newark the taxis are organised and dispatchers will ask you for your destination, then quote you the fare ranging from $50 (Battery Park to W 23rd St) to $70 (above W 185th St). Tolls and tips are extra, and there is an additional payment for each piece of baggage that is over 61cm (24in). There is no subway station for Newark.

The **Air Train Service** (*tel: (888) 397 4636; www.airtrainnewark.com*) links the airport with the Rail Link Station, from where New Jersey Transit commuter trains connect with various New York stations.

SuperShuttle Manhattan (*tel: (212) 209 7000 or (212) 258 3826 or (800) 258 3826; www.supershuttle.com*) provides a shared-ride van service 24/7 to anywhere between Battery Park and 227th Street, including major hotels. Advance booking is not necessary but can be done on their website or by phone.

The **Newark Liberty Airport Express** (*tel: (908) 354 3330; www.coachusa.com/olympia*) runs regular services to Grand Central, the Port Authority and Bryant Park/Fifth Avenue.

New York Helicopter (*tel: (212) 361 6060; www.newyorkhelicopter.com*) offers frequent flights from and between all airports to the E 34th Street Heliport at First Avenue.

By sea

Cruise-ship passengers arrive either in mid-Manhattan at the New York Terminal, which extends from 48th to 52nd streets, or at the Brooklyn Cruise Terminal in Red Hook (*www.nycruise.com*). Both terminals are air-conditioned and have streamlined baggage-handling and customs facilities. There are bus connections to midtown from the New York Terminal.

By rail

Long-haul services (Amtrak), New Jersey Transit and Long Island Railroad trains use Penn Station as a terminal. Local and commuter services use both Penn and Grand Central Station.

By bus

The Port Authority Bus Terminal at Eighth Avenue, between 40th/42nd streets, handles long-distance and commuter services (*tel: (212) 564 8484; www.panynj.gov*).

Children

New York's subways and buses are free for children under 112cm (44in) tall. Babysitting services can usually be arranged through your hotel, or through such agencies as The Baby Sitters' Guild (*60 E 42nd St. Tel: (212) 682 0227; www.babysittersguild.com*).

Climate

The city's climate is described as temperate, a fact many will contemplate

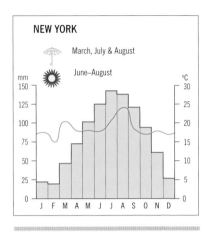

NEW YORK

March, July & August

June–August

WEATHER CONVERSION CHART

25.4mm = 1 inch

°F = 1.8 × °C + 32

ruefully at each end of the weather spectrum: in January, when the mean temperature is 0°C (32°F), and July, when the streets are stickily humid in an average temperature of 25°C (77°F).

Crime

Like any large city, there is petty crime in New York and strangers can be easy prey. The best way to avoid being mugged is to avoid lonely, dark places. Try not to travel on the subway late at night on your own or go into deserted parts of Central Park. Never carry more money than you are likely to need when you go out. If you do get mugged and/or robbed, call a cab and ask to be taken to the nearest police station. The police will file a report, which will help with any insurance claim you may make.

Customs regulations

The duty-free allowances for non-US residents over the age of 21 are 200 cigarettes, or 50 cigars, or 1kg (2.2lb) of tobacco or any proportionate combination; one litre of spirits or wine, and up to $800-worth of duty-free gifts (including up to 50 cigars), provided the traveller is staying in the USA for at least 72 hours. Articles should not be gift-wrapped. Prohibited goods include meat and meat products, dairy products, fruit, plants, seeds, drugs, lottery tickets and obscene publications.

Discount tickets

Entertainment in New York is not cheap, but you can reduce the cost. Half-price tickets for Broadway and Off-Broadway shows are sold on the day of performance at TKTS booths (*www.tdf.org*) in

High-rise parking

Times Square and near Borough Hall in Brooklyn.

The main booth, in Times Square, starts selling tickets for that day's matinees at 10am, but queue early to avoid disappointment. Tickets for evening performances are available from 3–8pm, Monday to Saturday.

The booths at Montague and Court streets in Brooklyn sell some matinee tickets the day before the performance. Opening time for the Brooklyn booth is Monday to Friday 11.30am–5.30pm, Saturday 11am–3pm.

Driving

If driving in the city is unavoidable, make sure you understand the restrictions, because penalties for infringements are stringent. In many streets, parking alternates daily from one side to the other, and it is illegal to park within 3m (10ft) either side of a fire hydrant. A car illegally parked will be towed away by one of the city's super-efficient contract crews, and the driver will be fined heavily. Never leave anything in an unguarded vehicle.

Breakdowns

Services of the American Automobile Association (AAA) are free to members of affiliated motoring organisations. New York City's branch is at (*1881 Broadway/62nd St. Tel: (212) 757 2000; open: Mon–Fri 8.45am–5.30pm, Sat 9am–5pm*). The AAA nationwide emergency number is *1 800 222 4357*.

Police presence on the streets is reassuring

Car rental

All the major rental companies have centres in New York, especially at the airports. Hirers will need to have a full valid UK or EU driving licence, and a major credit card or hefty cash deposit. They must also be at least 25 years old (only 21 if you rent in New Jersey or Connecticut). Car rental is not cheap, but some discounts exist for weekend rentals. Make car reservations before entering the USA for the best deal. Ensure that you are covered for liability to third parties in a driving accident, either by purchasing insurance from the rental company, or by taking out top-up insurance from your travel agent. Ordinary travel insurance does not provide this cover.

Fuel

The American pint is 20 per cent smaller than the imperial measure, which means five gallons of petrol ('gas') is about 18 litres or four UK gallons. Petrol is about half the UK price, and gas stations, many of which stay open 24 hours, usually require payment before allowing you to fill up.

The law

Drive on the right, do not exceed the speed limits, and do not drink and drive. Alcohol belonging to the driver or passengers must be kept in the boot. The upper speed limit on interstate highways in New York State is 105km/h (65mph), but lower limits may apply on other types of road. The city limit is 48km/h (30mph) unless otherwise indicated. Seat belts are compulsory. Passing a stopped school bus (usually yellow with flashing red lights) is illegal, and stiff fines can be imposed.

Electricity

110–15 volts AC, 60 cycles AC. Sockets ('outlets') take plugs with two flat-pin connections.

Embassies and consulates

Australian Consulate
150 E 42nd St. Tel: (212) 351 6500; www.australianyc.org
Irish Consulate
345 Park Ave. Tel: (212) 319 2555; www.consulateofirelandnewyork.org
UK Consulate
845 3rd Ave. Tel: (212) 745 0200; www.ukinusa.fco.gov.uk

Emergency telephone numbers

Ambulance, fire brigade or police: *911.*
Medical emergencies: *(212) 737 1212.*
Dental emergencies: *(800) 336 8478.*
MasterCard loss or theft: *(800) 307 7309.*

Thomas Cook traveller's cheques loss or theft (report within 24 hours): *(800) 223 7373.*

Entertainment information

Village Voice, published Wednesdays and available free of charge, lists all New York entertainments, as does the Weekend section of Friday's *New York Times*. Other sources: *Time Out New York*, *New Yorker* and *New York Magazine.*

Health

Vaccinations are not required for entry into the United States, but visitors are strongly advised to take out medical insurance cover. Doctors are listed in the *Yellow Pages* under 'Clinics' or 'Physicians and Surgeons'. Emergency departments open 24 hours a day:

Bellevue Hospital
4621st Ave at E 29th St.
Tel: (212) 562 4141;
www.nyc.gov
New York Presbyterian Hospital/
Weill Cornell Medical Center
525 E 68th St. Tel: (212) 746 5454;
www.nyp.org
Mount Sinai Hospital
1 Gustav L Levy Pl. Tel: (212) 241 6500;
www.mountsinai.org
You can also call: **NY Hotel Urgent Medical Services** (*tel: (212) 737 1212*). AIDS is a big problem in New York City, as it is worldwide, and the need to practise safe sex cannot be over-emphasised.

Insurance
Travel

You should take out personal travel insurance before leaving, from your travel agent, tour operator or insurance company. It should give adequate cover for medical expenses, loss and theft, personal liability (but liability arising from motor accidents is not usually included – *see below*) and cancellation expenses. Always read the conditions, which include any exclusions and details of cover, and check that the amount of cover is adequate. Remember that medical treatment can be very expensive in the USA.

Driving

If you hire a car, collision insurance, often called collision damage waiver or CDW, is normally offered by the hirer, and is usually compulsory. Check with your own motor insurers before you leave, as you may be covered by your normal policy. If not, CDW is payable locally, and may be as much as 50 per cent of the hiring fee. Neither CDW nor your personal travel insurance will protect you from liability arising out of an accident in a hire car, for example if you damage another vehicle, or injure someone. If you are likely to hire a car, you should obtain such extra cover, preferably from your travel agent or other insurer before departure.

Maps and guides
New York City's Official Visitor Information Center *810 Seventh*

Ave/between 52nd and 53rd sts.
Tel: (212) 484 1222; www.nycgo.com.
Open: Mon–Fri 8.30am–6pm, Sat & Sun
9am–5pm, holidays 9am–3pm. The
centre has information on almost
everything that goes on in the city, as
well as transport and accommodation
details. Street maps are sold in
bookshops, and easy-to-use
laminated maps can be purchased
for under $6.

Measurements and sizes

The USA uses imperial measurements.

Media

The *New York Times* is a multi-section
broadsheet with daily and Sunday
editions. The city has two tabloids, the
New York Post, which likes to
sensationalise things, and the *Daily
News*. The only national daily
newspaper is *USA Today*, but in New
York the *New York Times* has more
impact. The *Wall Street Journal*, New
York-based, carries national and
international news as well as financial
reports. For the visitor, *New York
Magazine* or the popular weekly
magazines *The New Yorker* and *Time
Out New York* are good buys.

Quality documentaries, plays and
educational programmes are on Public
Broadcasting Services' Channels
Thirteen/WNET, WLIW21 and NJN
Public Television.

The most popular cable TV
programmes are the 24-hour Cable
News Network, the films on HBO

CONVERSION TABLE

FROM	TO	MULTIPLY BY
Inches	Centimetres	2.54
Feet	Metres	0.3048
Yards	Metres	0.9144
Miles	Kilometres	1.6090
Acres	Hectares	0.4047
Gallons	Litres	4.5460
Ounces	Grams	28.35
Pounds	Grams	453.6
Pounds	Kilograms	0.4536
Tons	Tonnes	1.0160

To convert back, for example from
centimetres to inches, divide by the number
in the third column.

(Home Box Office), and music on
MTV (Music Television).

Some useful websites are:
www.mta.info Home page for the
Metropolitan Transportation Authority,
running New York transport systems;
www.nycgo.com New York City's official
tourism website; *www.nylovesu.co.uk*
New York State's official tourism
website; *www.allnewyorkhotels.net*
Comprehensive hotel booking website;
nymag.com Full city coverage on a
wonderfully comprehensive website
from *New York Magazine*.

Money matters

A dollar is made up of 100 cents, with
coins of 1 cent (a penny), 5 cents
(nickel), 10 cents (dime), 25 cents
(quarter) and one dollar. The quarter is
the most useful coin for slot machines,
telephones and parking meters.
Dollar bills come in denominations of
1, 2, 5, 10, 20, 50 and 100, and they are
all exactly the same in size and colour,

except that each carries a portrait of a different US president. Any amount of dollars may be imported or exported, but amounts larger than $10,000 – in cash or gold – must be reported to US Customs.

Currency exchange offices, banks and automated teller machines (ATMs) are widely available throughout all three New York airports, and everywhere in the city.

Thomas Cook traveller's cheques are readily recognised in New York, and accepted for encashment or transactions in most hotels and many shops. But you should make sure that they are US currency cheques.

Banking hours are usually Monday to Friday 9am–4pm. Some banks stay open later on Fridays, or open on Saturday mornings.

The USA runs on plastic money, and 'major credit cards' are a requirement when checking into a hotel, or renting a car. Cards can also be used in ATMs.

National holidays
Busy holiday times:
1 January New Year's Day
January, second Monday Martin Luther King Day
February, third Monday President's Day
May, last Monday Memorial Day
4 July Independence Day
September, first Monday Labor Day
October, second Monday Columbus Day
11 November Veterans' Day

November, fourth Thursday Thanksgiving
25 December Christmas Day

Organised tours
The best way to get the most out of New York is to tour on foot, and a number of companies and special-interest organisations exist which arrange walking tours for groups, usually led by an expert in a particular area or subject.

There are legions of companies giving walking tours in the city. Get a copy of the Official NYC Guide (via local New York tourist offices or check online www.nycvisit.com).

The Bronx County Historical Society (tel: (718) 881 8900; www.bronxhistoricalsociety.org) and Brooklyn Historical Society (tel: (718) 222 4111; www.brooklynhistory.org) both lead strolling tours of the highlights of their respective areas.

In Central Park the Urban Rangers (tel: (212) 427 4040) organise a year-round programme of free educational walking tours.

Various companies specialise in tours of Harlem. Harlem Your Way (tel: (212) 690 1687; www.harlemyourwaytours.com) offers tours that cater to special interests, including Sunday church visits, jazz walks or general interest. More specific but still fun, The Enthusiastic Gourmet (tel: (646) 209 4724; www.enthusiasticgourmet.com) introduces tastes and flavours of the city via food shops and restaurants, interspersed with local history.

Bus tours

Gray Line (*tel: (212) 445 0848; www.newyorksightseeing.com*) has been conducting tours of New York for more than half a century, and its current selection of about 25 tours covers everything from a trip to Radio City Music Hall to journeys up the Hudson Valley and to the casinos of Atlantic City in New Jersey.

Boat tours

Circle Line (*tel: (212) 563 3200; www.circleline42.com*) offers a three-hour circumnavigation of Manhattan Island. Trips operate from the Hudson River end of 42nd Street several times a day. Cheapest of all, of course, is the free Staten Island Ferry.

Helicopter tours

Liberty Helicopter Tours (*tel: (212) 967 6464; www.libertyhelicopter.com*) offers breathtaking day- and night-time flights.

Pharmacies

Medication for minor ailments and injuries can be obtained at pharmacies, found on almost every block. They also sell a wide range of cosmetics, toiletries, sanitary items and contraceptives. Usual opening hours are 9am–6pm, Monday to Saturday, but 24-hour service is provided at many Duane Reade (*www.duanereade.com*) and CVS (*www.cvs.com*) locations.

No, not the wrong picture – just a bus tour of New York

Places of worship

New York has more than 2,500 places of worship, and every religious denomination is represented. Look in the *Yellow Pages*, or ask the concierge at your hotel.

Police

Police headquarters are in the Civic Center. In an emergency, dial 911 or use one of the clearly marked street police telephones which have a direct line to emergency services. There are precinct (district) police stations all over the city. To find the nearest, dial *(646) 610 5000.*

Post offices

Stamps can be purchased in shops, supermarkets and at hotel reception desks. Post offices are scattered throughout the city, with the main branch at Eighth Avenue/33rd Street on the West Side (*tel: (212) 967 8585*). It is open 24 hours a day, Monday to Saturday. Poste Restante ('c/o General Delivery' is the American term) should be addressed to the General Post Office, 321 Eighth Avenue, NY 10001. Two forms of identification need to be produced when collecting mail.

Public transport

Contact the MTA Information Bureau (*tel: (718) 330 1234; www.mta.info*), which is available 24 hours a day for transport information. Maps are available from the information booth at

Police truck designed to cope with big-city traffic

Grand Central Station or the New York Convention and Visitors' Bureau at 2 Columbus Circle.

Bus

About 40 services run in Manhattan, mostly running north–south along the avenues, with crosstown (east–west) services every ten blocks or so. Bus stops are indicated by red, white and blue poles marked with route numbers. Enter at the front and pay a flat fare; drop the exact money into the fare box or use a Metrocard. If you need to change buses, ask the driver for a free Addfare ticket.

Subway

The subway is the best way to get around New York. Express trains 'leapfrog' several stations at a time, while 'locals' stop at each one. A route map is displayed in each carriage and can also be easily obtained free of charge by request at any subway token booth. Passengers buy Metrocards of varying denominations (put $8 or more on a Metrocard and get a 15 per cent bonus). You can also obtain discounted daily, weekly, monthly or pay-per-ride cards at token booths or vending machines at subway stations.

Driving near Central Park

There are also 1-, 7- and 14-day unlimited passes available. These cards generally provide the easiest and cheapest way to travel via city buses and subways.

Taxis

Hail or wave when you see a cab displaying an illuminated 'available' sign. Fares are metered, with surcharges for weekend and night-time trips.

Trains

Amtrak (*tel: (212) 630 6400 or 1 800/872 7245 toll free*) serves stations to the north and south of the city from both Grand Central and Penn stations. The Long Island Railroad (*tel: (718) 217 LIRR*) serves destinations in Queens, and both the north and south shores of Long Island from Penn Station. Port Authority Trans-Hudson (PATH) provides commuter services to Newark, Jersey City and Hoboken in New Jersey from stations in Manhattan (*tel: (800) 234 7284*). The Thomas Cook Overseas Timetable provides details of local and intercity trains, as well as long-distance buses.

Senior citizens

Many hotels offer discounts of up to 50 per cent off rack rates, and most of New York City's top attractions have special rates and services for seniors.

Student and youth travel

Students can get discounts in many attractions, but will need to show proof of their status. (*For YMCA and hostel details, see pp174–5.*)

Sustainable tourism

Thomas Cook is a strong advocate of ethical and fairly traded tourism and believes that the travel experience should be as good for the places visited as it is for the people who visit them. That's why we firmly support The Travel Foundation, a charity that develops solutions to help improve and protect holiday destinations, their environment, traditions and culture. To find out what you can do to make a positive difference to the places you travel to and the people who live there, please visit *www.thetravelfoundation.org.uk*

Telephones

It's worth remembering that anywhere outside the *212* and *646* code area – Manhattan – is a long-distance call. The other boroughs are in the *718* area. Phone booths are frequently hard to find. They take quarters, and a local call costs 25 cents for the first three minutes. For anything other than a local call dial *1*, then the area code.

For overseas calls it is much cheaper – and often quite reasonable – to use prepaid phone cards available in local shops around town (look for their advertisements in the window). First dial *011* then the country code, followed by the local code without the initial zero, and finally the local number.

Country codes:
Australia *61*
Canada *1*
Ireland *353*
New Zealand *64*
UK *44*
For directory enquiries in New York dial *411*.

Tipping

Cab drivers now expect a few dollars more than the fare, waiters and waitresses should get 15 per cent minimum, and hotel porters at least $1 per bag.

Travellers with disabilities

Public buildings, pavements (sidewalks) and buses (the newer ones, at least) have all been modified to accommodate wheelchairs. But some subway stations and most taxis remain no-go areas for visitors with disabilities. Information can be obtained from the Disabilities Office (*tel: (212) 788 2830*) or the Access Coordinator (*tel: (212) 669 3602; www.iloveny.state.ny.us*).

For reduced fares, call MTA Transit's Travel Line for People with Disabilities (*tel: (718) 596 8585*). For door-to-door services, call Access-a-Ride (*tel: (718) 694 3581*).

The New York Division of Tourism, *1 Commerce Plaza, Albany, NY 12245* (*tel: (800) 225 5697*), and the New York State Parks Department, *Albany, NY 12238* (*tel: (518) 474 0456*), can provide information on facilities for travellers with disabilities.

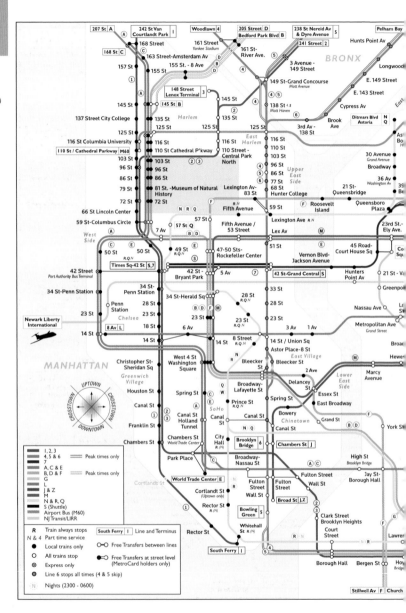

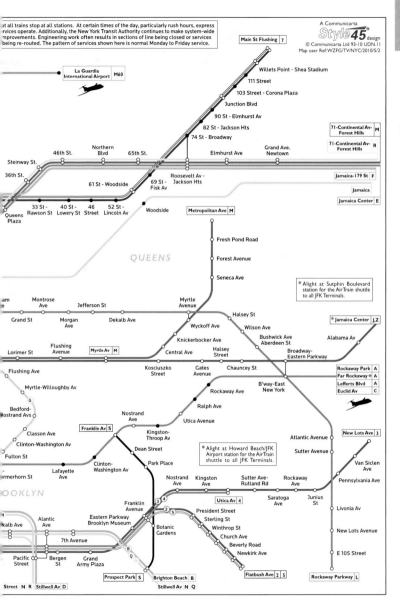

Index

A

Abyssinian Baptist Church 90
accommodation 172–5
African American Museum 116
airports and transfers 176–7
Alice Austin House 126, 127
American Folk Museum 62
American Museum of Natural History 79–80, 149
American Museum of the Moving Image 118–19, 147
American Numismatic Society 34
Apollo Theater 90
Asia Society 80
Astoria 146

B

ballet and dance 142
banks 183
Barrett Park 127
Bartow-Pell Mansion 100
Battery Park 30, 34
Battery Park City 60
beaches 132
Bear Mountain State Park 137
boat tours 134, 184
Borough Hall 108
botanical gardens 108, 122, 130, 133
Bowery 36
Bowling Green 30
Bowne House 119–20
bridges and tunnels 22–5
Brighton Beach 108, 132
Broadway 50–51, 54, 59, 76–7
Bronx, The 6–7, 100–7, 169–70, 183
Bronx Heritage Trail 101
Bronx Museum of the Arts 101
Bronx Supreme Court House 101
Bronx Zoo 101–2, 149
Brooklyn 7, 108–15, 110–11, 170–71
Brooklyn Academy of Music 108
Brooklyn Botanic Garden 108, 133
Brooklyn Bridge 22–3, 34, 108
Brooklyn Children's Museum 108–9
Brooklyn Heights Historic District 109, 110–11
Brooklyn History Museum 109

Brooklyn Museum of Art 109
brownstone houses 66
buses 178, 184, 185

C

car rental 180
Carl Schurz Park 98
Carnegie Hall 62, 64, 143–4
Carnegie Hill 99
Castle Clinton 30, 34
Cathedral Church of St John the Divine 80
Central Park 81–3, 86–7, 148–9
Central Park Zoo 83, 148–9
children 178
children's attractions 148–9
Children's Museum of Manhattan 83, 148
Children's Zoo 148
Chinatown 15, 36–7
Chrysler Building 5, 64
Church of the Ascension 44, 47
Church of the Holy Trinity 98–9
Church of the Transfiguration 34, 37, 64–5
cinema 146–7
Citi Field 120
Citicorp Center 65
City Hall 13, 34, 35
City Hall Park 54
City Island 102
classical music and opera 142–4
Clay Pit Ponds Park 127
climate and seasons 178
The Cloisters Museum 83
Cloves Lake Park 127
Cobble Hill 109, 113
Cold Spring Harbor Whaling Museum 116
Coney Island 109, 132, 148
Conference House 127
Connecticut 136
conversion table 182
Cooper-Hewitt Museum 83, 99
Cotton Club 90
Court Quarter 54
Cradle of Aviation 116
credit cards 183
crime 178
cruise ships 178
Custom House 30
customs regulations 179

D

Diamond District 65
disabilities, travellers with 187

discount tickets 179
driving 179–80, 181
Dyckman House 88

E

East Village 40–41, 42–3
eating out 156–71
El Museo del Barrio 88
electricity 180
Ellis Island 35, 38
embassies and consulates 180
emergency telephone numbers 180–81
Empire State Building 5, 65, 68
Enrico Fermi Cultural Center 102
entertainment 142–7, 181

F

farmers' markets 158
Federal Hall 38
Federal Reserve Bank of New York 39
festivals and parades 16–17
Flatiron Building 67
Flushing Meadows-Corona Park 120
food and drink 156–71
Forbes Magazine Galleries 39
Fordham University 102
Fort Tryon Park 134
Fraunces Tavern Museum 30–31, 39
Frick Collection 88
Friends' Quaker Meeting House 120
Fulton Ferry Landing 110, 114

G

Garibaldi-Meucci Museum 127–8
Garvies Point Museum and Preserve 116
Gateway National Recreation Area 121, 128
gay and lesbian scene 47, 167
George Washington Bridge 22, 23
Gracie Mansion 88, 98
Grand Central Station 68–9
Grant's Tomb 88–9
Green Belt 128
Greene Street 51
Greenwich Village 39, 42, 44–5, 46–7
Greenwood Cemetery 114, 133–4
Grey Art Gallery 44
Ground Zero 61
Guggenheim Museum 89, 99

H

Hall of Fame for Great Americans 102
Hamptons, The 136
Harbor Defense Museum 114
Harlem 89–91, 183
Harlem Walk of Fame 90–91
Hayden Planetarium 79–80
health 181
helicopter tours 184
Henderson Place Historic District 98
High Line 69
history 8–10, 124–5
Hudson Valley 137
Huntspoint Historic District 123

I

Immigration Museum 38
insurance 181
International Center of Photography 69
Intrepid Sea-Air-Space Museum 69
Inwood Park 134

J

Jacob Riis Park 132
Jacques Marchais Center of Tibetan Art 129
Jamaica Arts Center 120
Jamaica Bay Wildlife Refuge 121, 135
jazz, blues and folk 144–5
Jefferson Market Courthouse 44
Jewish Museum 91
Jones Beach State Park 132, 135

K

Kingsland Homestead 121
Kissena Park 134

L

LaGuardia Community College Archives 121
Lefferts Homestead 114
Lehman Center for the Performing Arts 102–3
Lincoln Center for the Performing Arts 85, 94, 142–3
Little Italy 37, 107
Little Odessa 108
Little Singer Building 50
Long Island 116–17, 136–7
Long Island City 123
Long Island Maritime Museum 116
Lower East Side Tenement Museum 45

M
McSorley's Old Ale House 40
Madame Tussaud's New York 69
Madison Square Garden 69–70, 150
Malcolm Shabazz Mosque 91
Manhattan 6, 7, 18, 28–99
  accommodation 172–5
  eating out 156–9, 162–5, 168–9
  Lower Manhattan 34–62
  maps 29, 63
  Midtown Manhattan 62–79
  shopping 138–41
  Upper Manhattan 79–99
maps and guides 181–2
Marcus Garvey Park 91
measurements and sizes 182
medical treatment 181
Metropolitan Museum of Art 95–6
Metropolitan New York 6–7
Metropolitan Opera House 94, 144
money 182–3
Montauk 136
Morgan Library 70
Morris-Jumel Mansion 96
Mount Vernon Hotel Museum and Garden 96
Municipal Building 54
Museum for African Art 96
Museum Mile 99
Museum of Arts and Design 70
Museum of Biblical Art 96
Museum of Bronx History 104
Museum of Chinese in the Americas 37
Museum of Modern Art 70–71, 147
Museum of the American Indian 30, 45
Museum of the City of New York 97
Museum of the Staten Island Institute of Arts and Sciences 129

N
National Academy of Design 99
national holidays 183
Nautical Museum 102
New Museum of Contemporary Art 45
New York Aquarium 114–15, 148

New York Botanical Garden 103–4, 133
New York City Fire Museum 45, 48
New York Hall of Science 121
New York Harbor 26–7
New York Historical Society 97
New York Public Library 15, 71
New York State Supreme Court House 121
New York Stock Exchange 33, 48
New York Transit Museum 115
New Yorkers 25, 92–3, 106–7
newspapers and magazines 182
nightclubs and discos 145–6, 166, 167
Noguchi Museum 120

O
Off-Broadway 76
Old Bethpage Village Restoration 116–17

P
parks 134
passports 176
pedestrians 19
Pelham Bay Park 104, 134
pharmacies 184
places of worship 185
Plymouth Church of the Pilgrims 111, 115
Poe Cottage 104
police 185
Police Academy Museum 48
politics 12–13
post offices 185
Prospect Park 115, 134
P.S.1 MoMA 121–2
public transport 18–19, 185–6
pubs 166–7

Q
Queens 7, 118–25, 171
Queens Botanical Garden 122
Queens County Farm Museum 122
Queens Museum 122–3
Queens Zoo 123
Queensboro Bridge 24, 25, 122

R
Radio City Music Hall 71, 72, 147
rail services 178, 186
Raynham Hall 117
Richmondtown Restoration 129–30

Riverdale 104
Riverside Church 97
Rockaways 123, 132
Rockefeller Center 71–3
Rockefeller Mansion 137
Roosevelt Island Aerial Tramway 19, 24
Rubin Museum of Art 48

S
safety and security 18, 19, 22, 178
Sag Harbor 136
Sagamore Hill National Historic Site 117
St Demetrius Cathedral 123
St Mark's Place 40, 42
St Mark's-in-the-Bowery 40, 52
St Patrick's Cathedral 74
St Paul's Chapel 52, 54
St Vartan Armenian Cathedral 74
Sands Point Park and Preserve 117
Schomburg Center for Research in Black Culture 91
senior citizens 186
September 2001 terrorist attacks 4, 32, 60, 61
Sheepshead Bay 115
shopping 138–41
Snug Harbour Cultural Center 130
SoHo 50–51
Soldiers' and Sailors' Memorial Arch 114
South Street Seaport 48–9, 52, 55, 149
sport and leisure 150–55
Staten Island 7, 126–31, 171
Staten Island Botanical Garden 130, 133
Staten Island Children's Museum 130–31
Staten Island Ferry 19, 26
Staten Island Zoo 131
Statue of Liberty 8, 52–3, 56–7
Strawberry Fields 86
Strivers' Row 91
student and youth travel 186–7
Studio Museum 91
subway 18, 19, 22, 186, 188–9
Sunnyside 137
sustainable tourism 187

T
Tarrytown 137
taxis 18, 186
telephones 187
Temple Emanu-El 97
Theater District 74
theatre 146–7

tipping 167, 187
Top of the Rock 73
tourist information 191–2
tours, organised 183–4
traveller's cheques 183
travelling to New York 176–8
TriBeCa 58–9
Trinity Church 31, 56, 57
TV 182

U
Ukrainian Museum 57
UNICEF House 74
United Nations Headquarters 74–5, 78–9
Upper West Side 84–5

V
Valentine-Varian House 104
Van Cortlandt Park 104
Verrazano-Narrows Bridge 23, 27, 131
Vietnam Veterans' Memorial 57, 60
Villard Houses 79
visas 176

W
Waldorf-Astoria Hotel 79
walking tours 183
walks 30–31, 36–7, 40–41, 46–7, 50–51, 54–5, 58–9, 86–7, 98–9, 110–11
Wall Street 31, 32–3
Washington, George 31, 52, 54, 125
Washington Market Park 58
Washington Square 42, 45, 46, 47
Wave Hill 104–5
West Point 137
White Horse Tavern 45
Whitney Museum Altria 79
Whitney Museum of American Art 97
wildlife 134–5
William T Davis Wildlife Refuge 131
Williamsburg 113
Woodlawn Cemetery 105, 134
Woolworth Building 54, 60, 67
World Financial Center 60, 149
World Trade Center 61, 67

Y
Yankee Stadium 100, 105
yellow cabs 18
Yeshiva University Museum 62
Yorkville 98–9

Acknowledgements

Thomas Cook Publishing wishes to thank the photographers, picture libraries and other organisations, to whom the copyright belongs, for the photographs in this book.

AA PHOTO LIBRARY (Douglas Corrance): 26a, 51, 67b, 89, 93a, 112, 113a, 113b, 161a, 170
AA PHOTO LIBRARY (Paul Kenward): 13, 17b, 19a, 19b, 22b, 23, 42, 56, 57, 67a, 72, 73, 80, 85, 93b, 107, 115, 119, 131, 133, 148, 160a, 160b, 161b, 184, 185, 186
ALICE AUSTEN HOUSE MUSEUM AND GARDEN: 127
DREAMSTIME: 1 (Achilles/Serban Enache), 38 (Gary718), 53 (Bradcalkins), 65 (Pixelstate), 71 (Mbastos), 82 (Stubblefieldphoto), 105 (Eddtoro35), 120 (Shiningcolors), 122 (Leesniderphotoimages), 151 (Afagundes), 167 (Phakimata)
ETHEL DAVIS: 11, 17a, 18, 22a, 24a, 25, 32, 33, 37, 43, 47, 48, 49, 59, 60, 62, 64a, 68, 70, 75, 76, 77, 78, 81, 84, 90, 94, 101, 137, 143, 154, 155, 157, 171, 174, 175, 179, 180
FLICKR: 27 (Phil Covitz), 92 (David Berkowitz), 103 (Jennie), 134 (Christopher Esposito), 149 (Dave Fletcher), 159 (ralphandjenny), 165 (Ian Wilson), 166 (flickr4jazz), 169 (Lauren Manning)
JULIE CRANE: 66, 86
KAREN BEAULAH: 24b
LEONARD HOSPIDOR: 15, 163
MARY EVANS PICTURE LIBRARY: 124, 125
SIMON BEAULAH: 5
STATEN ISLAND MUSEUM COLLECTION: 129
WIKIMEDIA COMMONS: 16 (Dschwen), 26b (Aude); 52; 74 (David Shankbone); 35, 88, 109 (Kmf164); 128; 173
WORLD PICTURES: 7, 8, 64b, 106, 123, 135, 145, 147

For CAMBRIDGE PUBLISHING MANAGEMENT LTD:
Project editor: Frances Darby
Typesetter: Donna Pedley
Proofreaders: Jan McCann & Michele Greenbank
Indexer: Marie Lorimer

SEND YOUR THOUGHTS TO
BOOKS@THOMASCOOK.COM

We're committed to providing the very best up-to-date information in our travel guides and constantly strive to make them as useful as they can be. You can help us to improve future editions by letting us have your feedback. If you've made a wonderful discovery on your travels that we don't already feature, if you'd like to inform us about recent changes to anything that we do include, or if you simply want to let us know your thoughts about this guidebook and how we can make it even better – we'd love to hear from you.

Send us ideas, discoveries and recommendations today and then look out for your valuable input in the next edition of this title.

Emails to the above address, or letters to the traveller guides Series Editor, Thomas Cook Publishing, PO Box 227, Coningsby Road, Peterborough PE3 8SB, UK.

Please don't forget to let us know which title your feedback refers to!